TYGERBURNING
LITERARY JOURNAL

LIBRARY OF CONGRESS
CATALOGUING IN PUBLICATION DATA
Marick Press
Tygerburning Literary Journal
Journal in English
ISBN: 978-1-934851-20-3

Copyright © by Marick Press, 2010
Edited by Jacqueline Gens
Design and typesetting by Marick Press
Cover design by Marick Press
Cover image: "Tantra" © by Liz Hawkes DeNiord
Printed and bound in United States

Marick Press
P.O. Box 36253
Grosse Pointe Farms
Michigan 48236
www.marickpress.com
Distributed by spdbooks.org

TYGERBURNING
LITERARY JOURNAL

―――――― Issue No.1, Spring 2010 ――――――

An Independent Journal of Poetry and Poetics

Edited by JACQUELINE GENS

Table of Contents

	Editor's Note	10
Jacqueline Gens	Year of the Iron Tiger	11
Nikoletta Nousiopoulos	Alpha	12
	Beta	13
	Gamma	14
	Delta	15
	Epsilon	16
Matt ulland	Poem	17
Stephan Delbos	In Belgrad burning Angels	18
Kazim Ali	Contract	20
	Application	21
	Convict	22
Barbara Paparazzo	The Red Silk Scarf	23
Eric Magrane	In the first years of the twenty-first century	27
Edith Södergren	Nothing	28
	A Wish	29
Steven Riel	Swimming the Contoocook	30
Ilya Kaminsky	11am Bombardment	33
	Tedna Street	34
	We lived Happily During the War	35
Cinnamon Stuckey	Languages	36
Sara Lefsyk	As if one were expected to pass through	37
	I said i wouldn't eat meat for stars	38
	now its time for the obligatory	39

Wendy Burk	*An Interior*	42
Dorinda Wegener	*Hinge*	43
Amanda Cobb	*On being Unsure*	44
	Last lost poem	45
Ann Marie O'Connell	*Let's wish it was 1938 or '39*	46
Nin Andrews	*The Beautiful Escape*	47
	The Book of Missing Nights	48
Alexandria Peary	*Tiny low garden*	51
	In the Courtyard	52
Miguel alejandro Valerio	*My brother's refrigerator*	53
Douglas Piccinnini	*Mode/Home*	54
Howard Faerstein	*Wasn't that a boy*	55
Joanna Penn Cooper	*Light as a Feather*	57
Mary McKeel	*Hummingbird and Shadow*	58
Maura MacNeil	*My Sister's Body*	60
Bhisham Bherwani	*My grandfather's Watch*	61
	Mother Tincture	62
	Ex Nihilo	64
Laynie Browne	*Scorpyn Ode*	65
	Departure	66
	Scorpyn Ode	67
	Departure	68
	Scorpyn Ode	69
	Departure	70
	Scorpyn Ode	71
Verandah Porche	*Ode to Of*	72
	Ode to an Adirondack Chair	73
	Ode to One Away	74
	Acute Ode	75
	Ode to Lavish Gestures	76

Tenzin Dickyi	*Four Rivers, six Ranges*	77
	Ingredients for the New Year's Eve Soup	78
	The Chorten	79
Lesle Lewis	*Life Flying Away*	80
	The Skeleton Inside the Flesh of the Young Woman Reclining	81
	A ferry Boat Ride	82
Adam Fieled	*Apparition Poems #1550*	83
	#1551	84
	#1553	85
Martha Carlson Bradley	*A*	86
Melinda Harr Curley	*Seed and Sparks*	88
Patricia Fargnoli	*Blue Woman in the Tub*	89
Mary Gilliland	*The Woman in the Hat Paused, Mole Eyed*	90
Tim Mayo	*The exile of your Anger*	91
Mark Watman	*Twenty Incantations*	92
Ivy Page	*Cherubim*	93
Terry Lucas	*Final Fitting Appointment*	94
Jane Lunin Perel	*Hospice*	95
Stephen Paul Miller	*The Content in a Joke is its Defense Mechanism*	96
	Pancakes	97
	Automative	98
James Harms	*A Wooden Horse*	99
Mariela Griffor	*Ripples: I enter the daylight*	101
	Chiloe Island	102
	The Tale of two uncles	104

George Quasha	Defining Gesture	105
	Configuring Principle	107
Brian Henry	Closet theater	128
	Food Court	129
	Snuff Film	130
	Mescal's Wager	131
K.A. Thayer	Curtis Byvarsky	132
	The Garden Variety Pneumatic Pigeon	133
	Escapade of the Unspoken	134
Leah Souffrant	Language about Language	135
Anchia Kinard	All that we are in holding	137
Sylva Boyadjan Haddad	Triptych-Dioscuri	138
	Homage to Dionysis	139
	Inconsolable	140
Chard DeNiord	World's Wild Fire	141
	From Box to Box	142
M.C. Jones	Flying & Misleading Moniders	143
Talia Katowicz	Espressioni per la tavola	144
	Ariadne	146
Tamara J. Madison	Solicitation	147
	Not only a Tupac Poem	148
Roberta Feins	Neighbor Trees	149
Alice B. Fogel	Variations 29:Boats	150
	Variations 10: Moths	152
Louise Landes Levi	Mr. Bliss	154
	Don't be	155
	Blue Bird	156

Lana Hechtman Ayers	*East Rockaway*	158
Erika Lutzner	*Cambodia: Sad Little Girls*	161
Kathleen Fagley	*Sadna*	163
	Suffer the Frogs	165
Lee Ann Brown	*But tenderly and with high math*	167
	Ampule	168
Laura Davies Foley	*The hands of Russia are long*	171
Janet Barry	*Spring Cleaning*	172
Barbara Loveneheim	*Fossil Fuel*	173
Tara Betts	*Marin County, August 7, 1970*	174
	Kent State, 1970	174
	Jackson State, 1970	174
Karen Dietrich	*Factory*	175
	Recurring Dream	176
Kent Maynard	*The Afterward*	177
Kyle Potvin	*Last Bite*	178
	Contributor Biographies	179

Editor's Note

The idea of using "Tygerburning" as a title emerged in 2003 when Chard deNiord and I were searching for a word or phrase that exemplified the essence of the MFA program in poetry we co-directed and founded together. Seven years later I am happy to present the inaugural issue of the literary journal, *Tygerburning* in the year of the Iron Tiger. Tygerburning remains in my mind an apt epithet for poetrymind in all its diverse manifestations.

Here are poems that leap off the page or as one contributor says, assert that it is OK "to color outside the lines." Like the tiger—the poets in this issue are bold, determined, assertive, hungry for raw meat, ever on the prowl for candor, sniffing the ineffable scent of the ordinary made extraordinary. I hope you enjoy this first issue of *Tyberburning Literary Journal*, the first of more to come with other guest editors.

Many thanks to Marick Press and the students, alumni and faculty of the New England College MFA Program in Poetry for their contributions and encouragement. Special thanks to Liz Hawkes deNiord whose painting "Tantra" (aka in Sanskrit meaning "continuity") offers a glimpse into the transformative 'ruined' portal into which poets courageously enter again and again to make sense of it all, or no sense at all, as is often the case.

Year of the Iron Tiger

Be prepared for uncharted fields
in the wild. Brace yourself to stalk
the prey of wandering thoughts
before you pounce
that old enemy—distraction,
all those frivolous wisps of hope and fear
hidden among weeds of mind.

                          Crouch low
Keep your nose to the ground

Smell wind
        Hear the rustle of ignorance
when hungry to ambush
that wildebeest of one's own rage.

Growl at adversity in the night
By day drink from the spring of Refuge
Flash your tiger's teeth at enemies
Guard your pride with ease among outcrops.

Then, let your steely gaze ignite the fire
of impenetrable essence –
                Awake in the blaze.

Jacqueline Gens
Losar 2010

Nikoletta Nousiopoulos

Aα
Alpha

There are as many alphas in the world
    as apple seeds.

Papou said
"find the star
    where seeds hide
dig them out with your fingernail"

Once, I planted seeds in my palms and grew poems—

Fruit puckered with its seeded core
whispered *alpha* in my mouth

taking over any notion of apple.

Ββ
Beta

walking the donkey by a rope
his ears make flutters of betas

flies, wings, and tired eyelids
beat betas on my face

and if my child loosens her
grip, of the gray animal she loves

bow ties and butterflies come
undone

Nikoletta Nousiopoulos

Γγ
Gamma

Give me an arm stretched to the East and I will follow until the fingers end and I am lost in the letter seat swinging

Δδ
Delta

I refused to explain holy
    water, swam
    scrapped shoulders &
bled a tear-shaped bead in the
delta stream.   Then
O Pappas

I was baptized.

Nikoletta Nousiopoulos

Εε
Epsilon

In America they prepare his body:
the (not) face, the half-a-rib
-cage, soul soft as detached petals.

Can they wash feet soft after reckoning
Kosmos, return him to village breath
-ing out ruins on mountainous curves—

Forehead & heart-place mark
the exit of body & soul, or
embalm what remains—

MATT ULLAND

Poem

We lived in the first century of total war.
Most days we didn't notice anything unusual.
In the mornings we would chew our cereal,
eyes fixed on screens that flickered smiles,
products, celebrity scandals. After awhile
we forgot what they were trying to sell us, who
was being sold. The morning papers grew thin
and shimmery as pixels. We were so entertained.
Now and then, a sunken-faced man
would stare. We were urged to stay indoors;
to fear neighbors, foreigners, everyone; to ignore
the acrid stench of gasoline, rifle reports.
We were living other people's lives.

after Muriel Rukeyser

Stephan Delbos

In Belgrade Burning Angels

On a bustling Belgrade street
corner, I heard the ghost
of Coltrane sprout like a fountain
from a busker's dented sax.

Two rabid-looking Arabs hocked
emaciated kittens;
calico and tabby bags
of ribs in a rusted cage,

and boiled ears of corn
from a garbage can.
A toothless woman sucked
and gummed the scrawny kernels.

Saturday night all over
the world and I was dying
for silence,
but Coltrane kept moaning

melodies through the medium
of a Serbian saxophonist wearing tattered
fatigues, with twittering
stumps for legs.

And stars shone down like holes
signifying whole notes
poked in black staff paper.
The half-moon seemed a deaf

conductor. I stood waiting
for a walk signal or augur
to guide me to the station
where I could catch the moving

stillness of a bus. The crowd
of shoppers and street merchants
swarmed me like an army
troop who'd traded uniforms

and horns for silver dollars. Laughter
should have been a comfort—
I could understand it though
I didn't speak the language,

but Coltrane was confusing,
retelling me America
beckons like a distant
flickering matchstick flame

also in the Balkans
where I had come for respite
but found myself the witness
to a butchered *Love Supreme*.

Kazim Ali

Contract

When sleep sends your name cannoning to the surface
    you let it go and plummet

from the sun to the ocean floor
    at the speed of crime

quoting decades of your shame's rosary
    turning in your hands their length of silence.

At the mosaic uncovered beneath the ocean floor
    you swear yourself a lifetime in which to speak,

then praying like anything your breath will last
    swim madly back up to the watery sun.

Application

Allowed across the yard, loudly complaining,
clamoring not for more room
but for a chance to take over
the chore of annotating
the categories of sin.

Sin equals a mid-spring snowstorm,
shame the direct result of lake effect,
Other transgressions include:

the death of your uncle of great courage,
a subsequent dearth of acceptable allies,
being sent to the placement office in unseasonable cold—

In the snow's loose registers you
log your disbelief and
strain to hear the rooms of time
assent to your application
drowning out
shame's white dismissals.

Kazim Ali

Convict

in the convicted evening I am a victor
struck loose and restless
creeping for the unlocked window

the family inside at the dinner table is mine
listening to the escape story on the radio
mother's hand freezes in the air halfway to her mouth

when she realizes it's me they're talking about
lightning by lightning the minute before thunder
the streets as empty as a beach

my hand on the cold glass
car alarm, tornado warning, catastrophe
who remembers the fugitive son

breaking curfew
when will the streetlamps go out
so my father can appear swiftly at the open threshold

beckon me quickly in

BARBARA PAPARAZZO

The Red Silk Scarf

Excerpts
[7]

Grand Trunk Road

Frommer's says whatever you do
don't go out after dark
in Bihar.

It's almost sundown,
       we're hours from Bodghaya
as a man in a red turban
ladles chai
into glasses and two skinny dogs
lie down
by the side of the road.

Tata trucks, bicycles, taxis, oxcarts
pass in clouds of dust.

Then
a jeep carrying men with rifles
swerves around a rickshaw —

how sudden
a malignancy appears.

BARBARA PAPARAZZO

[8]

Kalka

Two children
in the Kalka train station
    coming to the window

of the Himalayan Queen
the girl barefoot
the baby naked
hands to mouths, back & forth

I'm on my knees
    begging forgiveness
as I glide past their world

[9]

Delhi

Almost robbed getting off the bus
in Delhi carrying two Tibetan
rugs Woody jumps out of moving
rickshaw big commotion
man backs up car opens
trunk a few inches from the rugs
I am standing on top of
Carolyn waves arms
runs across alley to guest
house door (where we are not guests)
concierge calls for two new
rickshaw wallahs &

      suddenly the knot's undone
we speed
out of the narrow labyrinthine
lanes of old Delhi past the crowded
bazaars the ancient mosques the Red Fort
we are lucky today yes lucky
the dust of centuries
in our hair & teeth
the yellow-green smog
a shroud
over us all

BARBARA PAPARAZZO

[10]

Varanasi

A black pearl dropped
by the gods, the river
carries rowboats past
the 100 ghats —
the laundry ghat, the bathing ghat
the worshipping ghat
the burning ghat
where bodies covered with marigolds
burn on pyres
then float
       in the water
ashes, charred bone
singed flesh
while pilgrims do ablutions
wash clothes, dishes
their teeth —
       the skin
is just another thin boat
holding its fragile contents
on the Ganges.

ERIC MAGRANE

in the first years of the twenty-first century

it is more than
             language
makes us human
what is it that I hear
what is it that I want
a poetry of geologic time
outside everything we know
when we are out
             on the edges
today's gods
in our own understanding
    a new arrangement
underneath the surface
    today's structure
        swirling light—

& shining history

    weighs less than

a spider

Edith Södergran

Nothing (Ingenting, ca 1915)

Be calm, my child, there's nothing,
and everything is as it appears: the forest, the smoke and the vanishing
                                                                                   rails.

Somewhere far off in distant lands
there's a bluer sky and a wall of roses
or a palm tree and a tepid wind—
and that's all.
There's nothing besides the snow on the branch of the pine tree.
There's nothing to kiss with warm lips,
and all lips will turn cool with time.
But you're saying, my child, that your heart is powerful,
and to live without meaning is worse than dying.
What do you want from death? Do you feel the disgust his clothing
                                                                                        is spreading
and nothing is more repulsive than death by your own hand.
We need to love life's long hours of illness
and confined years of longing
as much as the brief moments the desert blooms.

                      Translated by Malena Mörling and Jonas Ellerström

EDITH SÖDERGRAN

A Wish (En önskan, 1916)

Of all our sunny world
I wish for a mere garden-bench
where a cat sleeps in the sun…
That's where I'd sit
with a letter pressed against my heart,
one single little letter.
That's what my dream looks like…

                Translated by Malena Mörling and Jonas Ellerström

STEVEN RIEL

Swimming the Contoocook

June 2006

Boys play at paratroopers
plunge   one   two   three   four
off the covered bridge   So far the drop
the angle of their limbs   crucial
as they knife midstream
We tsk at their sense of safety

One   two   middle-aged men
we pad our flip-flops
down a pea-stone path
to barely a beach
strip down to Speedos
another kind of risk

Main Street traces riverbank
and lining sidewalks today   countless flags
some stuck into lawns like pinwheels
some stapled   some hanging from fists
as the hearse slides by
Corners of bigger flags twined into chain link
along the overpass   where Magic-Markered top sheets
flap   "Thank you, Russell, for protecting our town"
at flatlanders speeding by

The boys sprint to where knotted rope
swings out from a branch
of a half-gone tree   its furthest reach
a third of this river's span

I think   *Boulder*   They think   *Blast*
They guffaw   yelp   soar out in twos
"You kicked me in the balls!" one pipes

We who have daily guided razors
round corners of our mouths
tiptoe past poison ivy to the spot
to slip in   You've volunteered
as lifeguard   and watch for bubbles
from snapping turtles

You've a baritone I could back-flip into
its New York burble smooth enough
if you weren't straight   if I weren't married
if we weren't actuaries
of granite beneath

In the runnel of sky unfurling
above the seam of this valley hamlet
above our backstroking hands
up where next week's fireworks will embroider the dark
Someone turned on the Military Channel
"Military ER"   *the show*
Tweezers grapple shrapnel
from a torso in Iraq
               I avert my eyes back
               to the glistening meadow beyond tall oaks
               to the roof of the Victorian library
               where mourners cling beside their cars
but blood keeps drawing my focus skyward
to the grunt's trusting eyes
I wonder where the remote is
who picked this channel

Abandoning the backstroke we strain toward the bridge
Kicking against the current as it ripples mid-river
I mark one tree to make sure I am moving
Our talk falls off for the effort

And finally we feel the luxury
of letting ourselves be carried back
towards boys   rope   all we grappled with
through summer camp's gashes
stitches   interrogations   before
we could become these two men
paddling together   and maybe
we'll help each other clamber up the steep
or offer a hand   at least

When we're done drying off
though constantly now
that soldier's childlike gaze posters my sky
I hesitate to ask
When you studied lifesaving
did they cover not just whitewater but dark
how to prop dead weight above the surface
how to talk about skulls
with boys who can fly

11 a.m. Bombardment

Stop talking while we are kissing!
— my wife hangs her underwear to dry quickly
    on the balcony as the helicopter circles

over Perki square, circles
over the women running into the fountain, running
    into cold water as if cold water

could protect the deaf women running
under orange umbrellas, under the chestnuts.
    We are in the street, we are

in the apartment again. Here are my
clothes packed in a bag on the floor
    where I sleep with my clothes on, I

feel footsteps soldiers, thinking, soldiers, thinking, soldiers—
honey, she is mouthing, I don't know what to do—
    her hand touches my ear, touches my ear.

If you can't stop these helicopters —
God of our brothers — helicopters
    in sunlight, policemen in sunlight

make them drink the sunlight
make them choke.
Take your chair outside, Lord,

    watch us run in this sunlight

Ilya Kaminsky

Tedna Street

On the balconies, sunlight, on poplars, sunlight. On my lips.
Today no one was shooting, there's just sunlight and sunlight.
A girl cuts her hair with imaginary scissors —
A girl in sunlight, a school in sunlight, a horse in sunlight.
A boy steals a pair of shoes from an arrogant man in sunlight.
I speak and I say sunlight falling inside us, sunlight.
When they shot fifty women on Tedna St.,
I sat down to write and tell you what I know:
A child learns the world by putting it in his mouth,
A boy becomes a man and a man earth.
Body, they blame you for all things and they
seek in the body what does not live in the body.

ILYA KAMINSKY

We Lived Happily During the War

And when they bombed other people's houses, we

protested
but not enough, we opposed them but not

enough. I was
in my bed, around my bed America

was falling: invisible house by invisible house by invisible house.

I took a chair outside and watched the sun.

     In the sixth month
of a disastrous reign in the house of money

in the street of money in the city of money in the country of money,
our great country of money, we (forgive us)

     lived happily during the war.

Cinnamon Stuckey

Languages

Those Mojave
Like to be cupped and washed
By the sand; bones blended with the bends
Of the river's lungs, we bead them up and slither
Down through the rocks
Wrap some red cloth aslant on our foreheads
As you look for us

We speak Southern Athabaskan,
We first raped Sonora in the 17th century
And her womb curved to our tongues,

Open on the buckskin, open against the earth
Face in pollen skirts
Face in the dust

Like a ceremony
Like a black sand ceremony
A white smoke ceremony curling through your hair

Do you remember who I am
Do you know who I am born from
Do you remember those bodies, over-arcing and pinned in the mud

Sara Lefsyk

as if one were expected to pass through
the enormous doorless place and take
the tiniest   uh   units along--impossible!

are you too afraid of trembling at the wrong times had been
     administered
as if one were to pass through the very heavy things and all   uh
at the same time   uh   your vital energies?

excuse us a minute while we have a breakdown nevermind
I can't tell what a building is pins in my homework ugh

we found universe on the median
lighting specs the buildings of therapy
help us levitate better help us plenty

this thing the   uh   swift dark darling thing light me I am on my
     way to therapy!
(to purchase the therapy and wear   uh   our weapons better the
     lessers indirectly)

let us put on our misery boots and hill some!

Sara Lefsyk

I said I wouldn't eat meat for stars unless they gave me breakfast first.
I never ate breakfast, you freaks, not breakfast! This is truly a psycho-spiritual club here, isn't it?
A not no one no church — agree?

Church is a roundabout way of saying "lunch" or "biscuits."

I likes my knives dull and in the real winter real winter i likes my knives you like babies club — agree?

Dear Eats Biscuits in the Rectory a While:

    when i say trace minerals fold over, fold over — agree?!

I likes me my minerals I am enormous knives a not one no lunch — yes!

Oh i am all terribly subconscious hehe.

now its time for the obligatory sign-in however
its frame of reference is a system of cosmology

my problem is   you ultra-moderns   you have absolutely
foot hills to each other circa
      does the nonidentification hurt much?   does not?

ok   and the terrible mass of actual trees?

nonsense! I too played a tabret once also
establishing a new repartee in the national public archives

Chapter Six: Soy Nails
in which we discover the highest common factor chemically per
      state capita circa

does the terribly absent particular doctrines   does not?

for another thing, we shook your doors is kind of us very much
she will never believe you

marma points a library full of tiny books an index card sequence
      biopsychospiritual structural organization

let us consider small pipes that lead upward
and make flow charts together

defiling motionless in the national public restrooms let us
supper this waterspout home a little circa

do the employees at the Bureau leak entrance by themselves
    much?   do not?

since this demonstration contains slides we should
thighs in the little cross section no?

ok   and the libraries of miniature dresses anyway?

what the heck? breaking entrance into the national public flea
    baths we found
reiki in the pie charts and   university professor?!

yes establishing a new american yoga in the national public flea
    baths   mundane

first of all I am worried about her myself also
having been more or less hemisphere

Chapter Two: Guruji, What Are Those, Devotees?
in which we discover absolutely evening tide and so but   take several often?

Wendy Burk

An Interior

Then, at that time: language.

Now: a table.

It's a place I closed my hands on

the multi-chambers of the head space

weren't enough?

Now: a window.

Now: a table.

Poems grow outside

nevertheless they need not work,

most though not all of the remembered **ONES**.

Hinge

In the room upstairs
a sturdy bed: marrow soft, filled
with the bodied smell of honeyed milk.

To be mother must mean to be wax
solidified over yield; to be the rubber
ring in Ball jar; the hinge on pantry door;

hymen then womb then symphysis.
The bearing says: open 90 degrees, let go 45.
Every morning, I wait for the bound

downstairs, the child's bid: toast with jam;
my desired movement for these two, set axes
occurs so fiercely in me, I fear: what now?

A return to carpenter, bee,
garden: my bed has been abandoned
for years, the bread consumed;

and as for my bony doorknocker —
that, too, shall decay: neither
fossil nor fruit preserved.

Amanda Cobb

On Being Unsure

A sign says "Welcome to the middle of a rope"
and there are fires and knives in here.
I conclude: nestle, photograph without a flash,
decide on god differently every day.

I learned I cannot tolerate
the boredom of absolutes.
When I joked of post-destination,
I became surprised for the first time
by raspberry eyes, juice and sweet-bleed —
— it took a long time to think of stains as colors.

My secret is:
filtering out the shame
by turning around three times
(one rotation for each dizzying bump)
and believing
in the scent of lemon in the stairwell,
the tap in the attic,
and whole towns, small, in the window well
of my empty house.

Amanda Cobb

Last Lost Prayer

This might burn, I have to think about it —

Yes, ever-present everywhere.
But you, "O Father,"
give me the mud suck of weeds by the side porch, a pact —
and after my part, several stages of shadow, peace with myself.
Instead,
a promise of space to straighten up from wild care
or enjoy the laying on of hands, then eyes, in public.
Crowns, plucks, and either/ors.

Across town, someone is prostrate
singing painful adoration, an obligation —
From me, a dare:
Omit omission.
Yet I share a bathroom with dirty cotton balls in the trash
and for a minute, nothing.
This afternoon I worry once about returning, supplanting —
Then I plan on mulch and suspect dahlias.

Annmarie O'Connell

Let's wish it was 1938 or '39
and someone (you)
was sleeping with me
in my backyard.
You can lie
8 hours a night
and be happy for a time.

You color the world
with petals
and water drops.
Someone (you) blooms
along every top row
along every balcony
in every one of my years.

These are things said
you know
merely words—

a place to be alone
sleep and move.

The Beautiful Escape

A girl learned to vanish at will. She could disappear, asleep or awake, and make the world go away. She could escape in a moment's notice, even when her parents were holding both her hands. Often her skinny freckled body would walk right out of her clothes without trying. But each time, it stung a little, just a little. After a while, she hardly noticed the pain. As the French say, partir, c'est mourir un peu. Even if escape can be beautiful, the loss lingers long after. Sometimes I see the her now, squinting back at me, as if expecting me to reach out. I worry that I will grow leathery and numb if I do not touch her soon. I worry what it will feel like if I do, but then she is always gone again. And again.

Nin Andrews

The Book of Missing Nights
after Jorge Luis Borges

I'm sorry. I admit I used your red hair and green eyes
in all of my poems where your freckled hand wouldn't stop
tracing my breasts, back then when I wanted every poem
to feel like the first kiss in the greatest lay I ever had.
That was years ago, once upon a time, when you were twenty-six
and I was a college girl, listening to Elvis's *Suspicious Minds*
and falling in love again and again for the first time. Let's just say
it began on a winter afternoon when you were wearing a black
leather
jacket, a cap and gloves, and were in such a terrible rush as usual,
you didn't notice when I slipped your *Book of Secrets* into my
pocket
after you told me not to touch it. Ever. Later that day,
I opened the book, and a red nude flew out and circled my head,
drifting slowly out of sight. I reasoned that all I had seen
was a scarlet leaf caught in a gust of wind. I was hung up
on Miguel just then, and he was tall and thin as a leafless tree.
He pretended to like me, but really he wanted to meet my friends.
That guy's a real asshole, you warned, and you were right.
The asshole wore a tan beret and never once kissed my lips.
The second time I opened your book, an old man with white hair
and a walking stick asked me directions to The Final Hour.
I told him to turn right at the corner of College Street
and Chagrin, then go straight to the Towers of Lost Love.
Or was it the Hotel of Others' Dreams? Who knows?
But that's where he saw us, lying arm-in-arm in the flowery
lit room where you kept lifting my crimson negligee
and circling my breasts with your tongue. When I glimpsed
a stranger's face in the window and turned suddenly

I only saw the mellowing sun. Or was the rising moon?
In any case, he was gone, and so were you. Outside Miquel
was laughing with my flirtatious room-mate, Sabrina,
and when I walked into the hall wearing a thick flannel
nightgown, I joined them for a glass or Burgundy wine.
The snow was beginning to fall outside, and its silence
was as soothing as the sleep of a red-haired man
who held me in his gaze all night at the Café Noir.
I could see him looking at me in the mirror as he sipped
his drink and nibbled a maraschino cherry. Before he left,
he came over to my table. His fingers brushed the nape
of my neck and traveled down my back and thighs.
He asked, *Haven't we met?* And said I looked just like
his sister. He wondered if he might have my phone number
and street address. Later I reached into my back pocket,
and your book was gone. Outside there was nothing
but a cold gray street, a drizzle of rain and sleet,
and a red stoplight flashing like the headache I suffered
the next morning. I woke up later than usual to the soft moans
of Miguel and Sabrina and suddenly remembered our plans
for a rendez-vous at your flat. You served coffee, aspirin,
and cigarettes. We stared at one another with red-rimmed eyes.
When your back was turned, I tried to slip your book
in my bag. It fell open on the floor and two Cupids
in mauve suits flew out and escaped through an open window.
They were instantly swallowed by the sky.
Perhaps they were cardinals. Or ravens. Or doves. Who knows?
After all, it was almost spring. Having bad allergies,
I began to sneeze, and you gave me some new-fangled pills
you said you'd purchased at the pharmacy. They knocked me out
for three days. When I fell asleep, a red-haired man
with green eyes caressed my breasts with pale freckled hands

to the tune of *Love Me Tender, Love Me Sweet* followed by *Suspicious Minds*.

tiny low garden
the tiny low garden in fine print
grows by repeating itself, the contractual maze:
there's a wait as though beside a blinking cursor
a bush with tea roses of sunlight
can happen twice in a row. I wake up and can tell
it will be a hot one. I raise my eye lids which are gritty tents
half-way up, careful not to disturb the purple mass
to my side that I have literally moved mountains for. Already off in
the middle distance where the mountains have been scraped away
in the middle no longer with mountains, the mountain-less
distance
people in catering uniforms are setting up the hedges
for the event in the garden. It's amazing how fast
the green bramble of vows throws itself on top of
compliancy. The entire screen occasionally flickers;
that doesn't surprise me as somewhere to the left
an indelible civilization is a mega-drain on resources.
I like the secrecy of my fringes, swish, elaborately long on the tents
and the watching of them without them knowing I am watching.
Six or seven inches longer than they have to be.
Now come the white dishes which clatter, the calla lilies
(of course this would be that bride's wish). Mesh of planning
that inadvertently catches a few birds thinking those are real
berries.
I guess it's fair to say that the wine critic is only a twisted tree in the
corner. A Timex?? Others appear to enjoy the contractual maze.
It is admirable how much fine print can be fit
into a narrow band daylight flirting in the cursive,
topped by gritty pearls in the morning
that is formatted on a small screen with thick black margins,
a picture frame balanced at the edge of a working stove.

ALEXANDRIA PEARY

In the courtyard

Some mauve words, some beaded trees
this part of spring overwhelms me,
each planted tree a comparison
done in seed pearls, a version
onto which strips of lilac felt are pressed
then held in place for a few seconds
above a generalized base —
as though created by someone skilled with a glue gun
& the types of detail I'm no good at.
I can't compete: what I've done
stands toward the back of the courtyard near the church wall
a few fuzzy words that I put there several years ago.
That one of the words has turned a shade of ochre
that's hard to come by — that I've been trying to put my hands on
for years —
purely by chance (plus exposure to a few
back-to-back winters) is most discouraging.

my brother's refrigerator

for Juan

my brother's refrigerator is crying he says
(the poor man's metaphor for hard times)

what kind of tears brother
is your refrigerator crying

are they blue like you will be
when they cut off your gas this winter

are they numb like the phone you've been babysitting
between interviews for the last three years

do they growl like your wife's stomach
in the middle of the night

do they smell like rotten meat
or are they clean like your son's diaper

30.X.'09

Douglas Piccinnini

Model Home

people wd like to act
like how they act
in real life in real life

for nothing's slow
novel cloud coating

when you know you
see an eminent you
framed daily don't

when you see the hand
shaped hand itself hold

its hair by its hair

Wasn't That a Boy

In mother's heart
desperate for a daughter, I was Helene.
Godmother Goldie dropped off a doll carriage;

no one raised a fuss.
Like Rilke in his dress,
wasn't that a boy?

The uproar sparked by my cross-dressing
would have been stifled
if instead of arch-rival

I was daddy's little girl.
And if I weren't a boy,
that summer afternoon in Brighton's shallows

might have readied me
for the disasters I've so often
carried into love.

Enter a stranger offering instruction in the breast stroke.
Looking back toward my brother,
crabs glistening on black rocks,

I take up position, stomach over his hand,
when fingers squirm over my penis
like a fistful of worms.

Quickly reconsidering, I frog-kick his blubber,
jump off and splash back to the blanket.

There was enough for me to do at eight

like imagining myself a father
without protecting my chastity
while swimming in the Atlantic.

Wasn't that a boy!

JOANNA PENN COOPER

Light as a Feather

It's true, I could be a lyrical child, kneeling under the dogwoods
in dappled light and breeze to channel messages,
when the air spoke in murmurs like dreaming.
Other times, I wasn't that. I lied about small things,
stole candy, pretended to sleepwalk, threw a plate of spaghetti
at the side of the house. I had a manual typewriter and used it
for yellow journalism and blaming notes to my mother.
I made up stories after lunch to spook the kids
at school, working at their minds until a chink opened. I did
strange magic at slumber parties, getting everyone
half-hypnotized and muted to the spot.
Light as a feather, stiff as a board.

Mary McKeel

Hummingbird and Shadow

You had a Golden Gate moon
Outside your window in your house on the west coast.
Then it got to be 2 a.m., and too quiet. A shadow came in.
A shade who made the ghosts in Dickens
Look like they came from Disney.
He said, "Here I am" and laid a pale, firm hand
On your shoulder, near your heart.
A tumor, an "oma", moved in.

A veil went over your life for a year.
Shell coverings that had held you,
Protected you in your formative years, fell away.
You grew expressive, but quiet,
So as not to stir up ghosts again.
Under the veil you found a fiercely beating heart.
You listened to its rhythm, and you learned
To hear the pulses of other lives

After the wave of disease and fear receded,
You found a refuge, and became a refuge for yourself.
You learned to see details.
Small things.
Like the hummingbird trapped inside, near the ceiling
Where his curiosity had led him.
You took your time.
With fingers like light breezes you freed him.

It took light fingers to win his trust.
You felt his heart beating, racing
As if pulling the adrenaline of twenty marathon runners.

You connected because you had felt fear too.
You had lain alone in a hospital bed with needles in you.
You still feel them, like the memory of a lost leg.

You and your friends debated whether the bird knew he was rescued.
Did you sense your own rescue when you lay in the cancer ward?
Did the doctors, the shamans, sense your colors?
Greens and reds through pale, wax paper thin skin?
Did they hear your heart, fragile, frantic and determined?

Maura MacNeil

My Sister's Body

For weeks she's run back
and gets so close I can see stray hairs
on the shoulders of her green wool sweater
and the sweat-wet curls behind her ears,
but as soon as she arrives
Maggie turns away to run back to where she's come
and I can't hear myself asking
her to come back to stay for once
over the sound of her leaving
to understand why she keeps running
back and forth —
and from what —
like she does.

When she comes to me like this:
so long-legged and breathless,
so weather-tossed,
so coltish and so wild in the eyes,
I think of miracles.

She survives like this
even since she's gone.

BHISHAM BHERWANI

My Grandfather's Watch

Cornell University, 2009

Grandfather wore the watch that I now wear.
Its luminous hands show time in the dark
and fall behind some minutes every day.
Its steel strap grips my wrist like a legacy.
I set its time to the time set in the landmark
clock tower on a college campus where
the illuminated dial at night carves
my years to date into almost exact halves.
Twice the age as when a student here,
as old as my grandfather's watch, no antique,
I wonder if youth is universally
lost on the young as it was lost on me.
My grandfather's watch has to be wound every day.
It ticks the way that old timepieces tick.

BHISHAM BHERWANI

Mother Tincture

Commonly known as poison ivy,
Rhus toxicodendron
has leaves that turn in autumn to
bright oranges, reds, and yellows
so dazzling that a vine that covers
a dead tree makes it look alive.
Its beauty notwithstanding, this
dreaded sumac infiltrates
orientations at summer camp
and, uneasily, dinnertime
chat otherwise agreeable.
Still, when it blooms in spring,
an herbalist well covered from
head to toe in jeans and long-
sleeved shirt and hat and gloves will pick
the green leaves in large quantities.
These weighed and ground and mixed with pure
alcohol and water in
precise ratios and fostered
for some weeks, until cured, produce
the remedial mother tincture.
Each succussion and dilution
cycle yields more potency:
the more dilute, the more potent
the liquid that sits in the dark
bottle in the homeopath's
clinic in Berlin or Bangkok,
dispensed ever so sparingly,
poison used to offset poison
ivy rash, treat rheumatism,

arthritis, anxiety,
elixir weaned and nurtured by
triumvirates of toxic leaves,
trinities of leaflets, and
Mother Nature, Mother Earth.

BHISHAM BHERWANI

Ex Nihilo

K. H. K. (1904–1986)

I take an empty space. I fashion it:
black-and-white-tiled chessboard floors, high ceiling,
bedrooms and anterooms, exposures facing
sea and trees ascending higher still.

I take the empty rooms; I furnish them
in sandalwood and seasoned sheesham:
armoires, tables, wicker chairs, and settees
between wrought iron and bamboo accessories.

I drape the tall windows with poplin curtains.
I crown the lamps of brass with shades of silk.
End to end with books I line bookcases, fill
sideboards with china and fruit bowls with fruit.

Palm leaves rustle outside in the monsoon wind
or summersault into the long veranda.
Salt crusts on walls around the moldings. Milk
boils on a gas stovetop inside the kitchen.

I breathe and breathe life into effigies
until you stir, Grandmother stirs, and, blind,
stirs your baby sister, my Great Aunt, and we
all pass each other in the quiet sunlight.

"A mind that broods over guilty woes is like a scorpion girt by fire"
—Shelley

"The Scorpion is an uncommunicative creature, secret in
his practices and disagreeable to deal with, so that his history,
apart from anatomical detail, amounts to little or nothing"
— Fabre, from *The Life of the Scorpion*

Scorpyn Ode

Skorpios, from Greek

(s)ker- "to cut"

Frugal, indifferent hunter

"taciturn creatures, shall I succeed in making you speak?"

Mithridates, king of Pontus accustomed himself to poisons

Lyk to the scorpion so deceyvable

Forget-me-not

LAYNIE BROWNE

Departure

From books from states from places from thinking one knows anyone, from erasure which was sent instead of smudged. From telling you. From the dark glass and from remarking or remaking after the hard falling. Departure from the floor, from accusatory remarks. From closing my eyes and imagining someone in your place. From someone in a dream who doesn't exist.

Scorpyn Ode

Babylonian Astrolabes, scorpion claw
45 degrees along the ecliptic
Serrated saw cuts through mountain
Releases underworld

Star of scorpion's breast, Antares

Sumerian Lisi, her name, written
With signs of brazier and red

Death dealing sting
Twin stars Sarur and Sargaz
Ur depicts an arm which reaps
Gaz, a mortar and pestle

Sun god scorpion with saw and scales
from an Akkadian seal
"Girtab," seizer, stinger, or
"Place where one bows down"
"Double sword"

Laynie Browne

Departure

From being elsewise aslant while we are lying upon assumptions. From *I must have it*. The "it" we must have taken as itself, whether it be person, book, meter, thing. Replace "thingness" with "hereness" and "hear-ness." Departure from not seeing them as they trot off into distant years. Meaning to clasp and to open and to close compartments which may or may not be fitting. From fear of signage and crooks escorting us carefully by the nose. From what are they after, all of these time-sensitive mailings? From bombardment. From meter reading and measuring. From the lost paper marking their height. From the tribe which says the name of one people is, and anyone else isn't. Meaning death to you is no insult. Departure from that thinking as a type of incision which makes no apologies for imminent casualties. From blankness as barrier, retort. From that odd way of hitting his head with the pencil when he cannot remember. From numbers which blind and besmirch. From wielding hoodlums, hoodies, hurdles. From provincial noodlers, bombastic ripped shams and disintegrated curtains. From, just leave it to me — nincompoop. From trouble of all kind, basically, stay home or I'll put you there. From thirteen feet of water under the bridge. From the circles under, bruises borrowing arms. From inappropriate questions. (After all we just met). From how the West was won.

Scorpyn Ode

Menologies, scorpion coincides
with seeding season
Favorable for the rise of oil and wool
Claws converted to scales as emblem of merchants

A child born in the 8th month will buy grain and silver
Dwellers by Euphrates
Associated the constellation with darkness

Artemis sent the scorpion after Orion
Egyptian Meretseger, Scorpion goddess with woman's head
Spit venom to protect pharaoh's tombs
Serket, "she who causes the throat to breathe"
Protector of the dead

Gilgamesh approached Mt Mashu
Scorpion folk divine he is only one-
third mortal and ask
Eternal one, why the long travail?
I seek my father Utnapishtim
No mortal has ever come
to know what you seek
So Gilgamesh set out and then over
transfixed by benevolent poison

Laynie Browne

Departure

From this place not beginning to begin, from beginnings are most difficult, meaning I'll just stand here and wait. Departure from the furniture resurrecting a dream in which beginning is another sort of trap, forsaking tapestry and topiary. Something is stopping or stunting. So you stand summoning numbers, careers, caricatures, cartoon manifestos of night. Standing against a wall resurrecting an orchestra of doubt or forsaken decisiveness recounting how she looked in a photograph, opposable. Departure from confusing a dinosaur with a raptor, from the repetition of dinosaur names, curmudgeons and colonels, dry recitations.

Scorpyn Ode

Scorpions strike the heel

Wherefrom the soul leaves the body

Children of Tiamat, dragon mother of the universe

Scorpion-man with bird feet

Falaknuma Palace of Hyderabad, India

in the shape of a scorpion with two pincers

Spreading out to the North, as wings

Perseus slew Medusa

Blood of her severed neck turned

To scorpions and snakes as it touched the ground

VERANDAH PORCHE

Ode to *Of*

Possession brands you
Cream of Wheat
Oil of Olay
    Duke of Earl
    Queen of Spades
    Jack-of-all-trades
'Tis of thee:
birds of a feather
in jaws of defeat
    Soft at the spin-off
    you quiver
    my lower lip.
No glove
dove shove
above:
    barehanded
    earthy
    levelheaded

Be
Love's
meek rhyme…

VERANDAH PORCHE

Ode on an Adirondack Chair

Repose on tilt
unbuttoned open-hearted.
Court sun.

    Skull loll against
    fanned slats. Flat arms
    warm slack hands.

Let the lake alone
scrawl and edit
with abandon

    ripple-pleat
    hillock
    conifer-speared air.

So fin-clouds
on boat-wake
dawdle

    till nightfall
    and the loon's
    transgendered aria.

Verandah Porche

Ode to One Away

Copper moon
beam down
on our twin solitudes.

>My ten
>loose ends touch
>type.

By the pasture spring
cicada courting
strum their abdomens.

>*I sha'n't be gone long*
>*Frost chimes.*
>*You come too.*

Acute Ode

Acid owns its sting
Acanthus a crowd
of thorns

    Acme the peak
    of excellence
    Acrid that weepy stench

Acrobats
possess
attentive strength

    Acuity is
    grief's
    barbed gift.

Acerbic
a cut to the chase
or quick.

    Ache... acute
    a call to arms
    our own.

Verandah Porche

Ode to Lavish Gestures

Equinox Sabbath
sun ruffles
snow.

    O
    spring, o,
    carpe diem.

Hold a candle
to the lay
of the land.

    Red hibiscus
    brandishes its
    manly stamen.

Her slim volume
skids toward his hefty
war memoir.

    Spectacles
    fog and link
    legs.

In the window
glint they turn
translucent.

Four Rivers, Six Ranges

The grim faced men in pictures
have a high glamour
that comes from afflicted nobility,
from close affinity with torn limbs,
burnt flesh, sacrifices and silver boxes
that are meant to keep
the wearer alive but do not.

Many of them are handsome,
strong-boned and laughter-lined.
In the photos they clasp each other's
shoulders, show their teeth
and face the camera with
black desperate eyes
that look and look at me.

If love is an imperfect translation of
the universe's longing for infinity,
what is hate?

Tenzin Dickyi

Ingredients for the New Year's Eve Soup

Cotton signifies gentility.
No, gentleness.
The wives of rich
Rinpoches have it and
fantastical nobility and brown doe
eyes of spindly-legged calves
and fire tested mothers' hands.
Cotton, and not the pea,
has to do with
tactile sensibility
and making love.
Butter brings you luck
the same way spilt
milk on doorsteps
the day of a journey
presages a good journey.
Your mouth will
be warm. Butter frustrates
the principle of frustration.
Butter you find in the mouths
of soft-spoken men.
Coal exposes a black heart.
These corrupting pieces
of carbon are only found
around trees tall
enough for giraffes
to hang themselves
from.

The Chorten

The chorten squats
in the mystery of
the incoming circle.

At five o'clock when
the pigeons flock, the
kora swells supremely.

A confusion of
men and women
asking only this:

What shall we do
with a love of
diminishing returns?

Lesle Lewis

Life Flying Away

You fight off feeling the suffering of others. You call your broken arm your army. You're King of the Third Floor. You can hear your food. You have a mood disorder. And a house and love disorder. We don't know what to do with you, and we have other worries too.

I want you to take off your pajamas. I want you to open a window for me. I want the back of your ear. I take a Polaroid of a Polaroid of a Polaroid of you at the city gates. Horses, cows, zebras, and giraffes graze within the city limits. Older citizens harvest what they can reach in the city orchards. The sooner we start over the better.

We leave a few girls and boys crying by the river. We commit strict and continuous self-examination. We try to take the friendly way in the shape of a walk that goes out, takes detours, wanders, and comes back a different way. Midnight and where are we? The house has opened itself but we're not in it or even hovering by the back door smoking.

The Skeleton Inside the Flesh of the Young Woman Reclining

Under the table in your living room in a box you've never seen before sits a perfect country house.

Make yourself a bower, put thee a statue and another vow not to whimper.

No one calls on you to do anything brave.

You have a new sweater.

Sometimes you are given enough to eat and sometimes not.

Are you saying you'll never be so carefree as to build a folly in the gardens?

A temple of modern or ancient virtue in ruins?

An atmosphere of fruitful melancholy?

It's not that you don't want to be of service.

Lesle Lewis

A Ferry Boat Ride

They think it impossible to live with such a constant awareness.

By morning the thought is banished and the ferry boat takes them back to the mainland.

How quickly there is great water between them and the island!

"It's a flag-waving perfect weather day for a ferry boat ride," they say.

They know that all is well not because it ends that way but because it is that way now.

Apparition Poems

#1550

I'm in your house:
your husband, kids
not home. A voice
(yours) follows me
around, playing on
my body, until I'm
in your bathroom,
smoking butts on

a sunny spring day.
Your body doesn't
appear. It seems to
me you're suspect,
Steph, it seems to
me you want too
much. Then, you
always said I was

a dreamer. What
do we have past
dreams anyway?
What else is love?

Adam Fieled

#1551

"Those who kill by accident
are not destined to be shot,"
so I feel no compunction as
to burying an entire city in a
hole at my feet; if it's hubris
(which it may be), then who
dies is just another bit of "I,"
expendable as broken rhymes,
excessive as a morality play in
blank verse, hokey as "moon
in June," so even as my rifle
accidentally fires perfectly I
can find something to relish
in the process: if there's two
kinds of precious, I'm one of
the good kind. Blue skies win.

#1553

I see her head, not yours,
on my pillow, dear, but I
don't really see either one
of you except as you were
when you had no interest
in my pillows: isn't it sad?

Martha Carlson Bradley

A

> In *Adam's* Fall
>   We Sinned all.
>   — New England Primer, 1727

Free of clothes, and private parts,
the human boasts a mop of curls—
and reaches out to calmly touch
one leaf, sleek as a viper's head.

The apple is hiding.

But the Serpent — a muscular
S — winds round the Tree
and grips, the tip of his tail
hovering.

        If it's Adam here
who's tempted to bite, where is Eve,
persuasive, her own misdeed
already done?

        If this is she,
spotless yet, the trunk of her body
more blank than a child's,

it's not Adam we see falling
to taint us all — though Sin,
nevertheless, is what launches
this stretch of lessons.

The wide-eyed Serpent
waits — his whole length flexed.

Melinda Harr Curley

Seeds and Sparks

Mother stares from her sink into our mill stack
yard of spent locust trees. Black branch smolders
against telephone wire. Cigarette smoke
yellows our enamel cupboards stocked
with chipped cups and plates and glasses that fly
from my father's hand and spark into shards
of light from the coke furnace of his rage.
Hot coals burst on the rug. Mother throws seed
after flower seed into dug-up dirt,
intends they grow no matter the soil.
Impatiens crowd marigolds crouched under
peony. Phlox squeeze between cement slabs.
Mother's favorite blooms orange only at dusk
against the odds in coal dust dark, like us.

PATRICIA FARGNOLI

Blue Woman in the Tub

after "The Tub (1886)" Edgar Degas

It's her shoulders you'll first take in, narrow, thin,
where she bends all the way forward from standing
in the shallow wide basin,

then the long angle of her back, bare, light's reflection
off it. One hand on her thigh as if for balance.
One elbow crooked, the other arm reaches

down with a sponge to scrub the tub
which no longer holds water.
A sheet's spread on the floor

to catch the wetness not there
when she steps out. Beyond, a corner of a chair
and a hazy window,

blue drapes sag from rods, drag on the floor.
She's young, auburn hair in a bun, but it's her bared
body that orders the work,

simple bold body, its tint of blue. Nude, she could be
any woman you'd see, in the middle of her life,
doing the ordinary tasks

women learn to do. She might be the whole history
of women who scrub clean a thing
after they're through.

Mary Gilliland

The Woman in the Hat Paused, Mole-Eyed

Then where is God?
The left side of the neck, the bottom of the big toe
We have plenty of stories
A shadow in the garden, a prejudice against the wolf
Forward without hesitating, not knowing whither
Not there? Any more than here?
We might be sick, blood loose in our entrails
Utilized in work, meticulously groomed and bathed
The hard tread of conversation, for example
Within ourselves?
Nowhere?
Hastening, going upstairs, staring across at the window
Remembrance torn in the sea wind swiftly, blindly

The Exile of Your Anger

If the cat greets me outside your door as the other exile
of your anger, her tail twitching at your contrariness,
the to and fro whip of your emotions, what should I
purr forth to please you? What sounds rumbling up
from the deep chesty cavity of my body can I throb
and thunder out if I am as heartless as you accuse?
Can even any sound come from such a vacuum?

Suddenly, I feel diminished before your door. I brush
against the cat's leg for commiseration. Strange triph-
thongs begin to mewl from my mouth. I become bereft
of the consolation of consonants: the absence of their clip
and purr preventing me to sculpt into the expressible
my un-wordiness. When will I regain my stature?
Recapture those *P*'s and *Q*'s I haven't minded till now?

Mark Watman

Twenty Incantations

She's the thick yellow eyes of the cat
She's deer blood on the pickup truck door
She's black-bone bone-ash china
She's vertebrates auctioned off the floor

She's birch-bark white as paper is white
      as bones are white and old
           and growing older

She dances the weaver dance of the snake

She's the cat's teeth pressed against my lips
She's the ugly arrow that messed your heart
She's toothless fate: vehicles driven and crashed
She's a shot in the head: he should bleed profusely
She twists the belt loop tighter

She's the check left there unbalanced
She is the prop of my distress
She's the axe of the imagination
She's married and seated in white

She is the way across that bridge

She's anonymous as bulk mail
She's bits of memory like bites on the neck
She spills the sea and washes away the girl
She is the year of the hole

Cherubim

Fat stupid angels
smoking cigars on the edge
of the bed. Ready
to burn my ashy toes.

These are not children,
they are dirty little men
that only care about keeping
the fat rolls around their
legs.

TERRY LUCAS

Final Fitting Appointment

Another customer in the three-way mirror,
Andre, the tailor, chalking up a two-button,

charcoal, Botany 500 suit — diagonal ciphers
begin at both armholes, follow tapered sides

down to the single, center-vented coat's tail,
signaling how much material needs letting out,

how many pounds gained since the wedding.
Tomorrow he will don this drab gabardine for her

funeral. She will be dressed in basic black
forever. The master tailor will take

care in shaping her earthen gown: it will mold
to her body no matter how much weight

is lost to maggots — proboscises probing seams
in pleated skin, unweaving flesh like needles

of millions of blindstitch machines gone awry,
their arrhythmic, electric voices even now

calling to the murmuring auricle in his heart.

Hospice

Carnelia cannot negotiate the cavernous silence of Opal's death. Even though Opal could not speak, she wrote everything down until her strength failed. Then Carnelia wrote everything down. When Opal lay in the hospice bed in her flowered smock, she was so alive, her eyes vivid, her gestures large. When Jade arrived the three sisters sat there, staring at the blue hydrangea Jade brought. Opal managed to write in her last burst, "What other blues?" Jade and Carnelia described blue blankets they had all slept under. The turquoise blue of their mother's eyes. Carnelia wrote a whole list of blues that night. Angora sweater. Ocean. Old Orchard beach Maine in noon sun, etc. But the next day when Carnelia got there with Opal's husband and youngest son, Opal was limp, her breaths slow. Gull wing slow, arching over the pier into the swelling waves.

Stephen Paul Miller

The Content in a Joke is its Defense Mechanism

We showed we didn't
need an alter image
to see into the world.
Against this backdrop
I've always had a little
laryngitis, I've never
been myself at all.
If you say the rhythm is put in
you speak as if out of the field or object.
If they crushed me I'd finger-paint with language.

Pancakes

Who's next?
I see a tall order.
Hey, it's leaping.
My character takes itself
seriously.
I love her.
We're cool with personal stuff
and get up to speed
but there's a bloodbath.
We're both being auctioned
and we are inside info
smelling each other's value;
our house is on a reverse
treadmill.
It's a beautiful lawn
going over the falls.
I go back
to get my *Seventeen*
where we skate
and slide to exurbia.
Can you sense humor
in my eyes?
The radio likes your taste.
Maybe we don't need the industrial
revolution anymore. I'm
off to Canada, then Cambodia.
If you can't reach me telepathically
try.

Stephen Paul Miller

Automotive

I might as well settle for what I always wanted,
                         the camel bells.
   You already know health, which is a kind
of intoxication
 before you meet yourself at a party
  and punch him in the face
the sea is sensed, like infinity to us, on
                         a beach.
Quite conceivably your stock drops, and
you look back longingly on the fact
             you can develop
 now because you didn't then.
 Grids defining words are
monuments that in turn are like
 eggs to egg salad, which
  like the horrid vegetable stew
    Jesus manages to spice just right
   for the women and take to the men
  himself is made
 into something the likes of which
no one had
tasted before.

A Wooden Horse

> "Oh bring it in and let us see it."
> — BSP

We tied ropes and pulled.
It rolled a little, and then enough
to cross the drawbridge,
which we drew back shut and locked
with iron rods. Nick and Sally
climbed the tower and crouched
low behind the parapet to take
their turns watching the east,
from whence cometh nearly
every one we've ever hated.
We'd heard the rumors and
knocked. But the thing was
all echoey and empty, though
inside we found flowers
and enough red wine to
tip the town into dreams
of poppies and fair
weather. Salvador sang
"The Ballad of Queenie
and Rover" while Ted sliced
the ham and spread mustard
on bread, and Evangeline
for once let down her black
braid and taught the kids
the cha-cha. We were ready
when they charged, daisies
behind our ears. "Whosoever

James Harms

steals will be blinded," Jamal
cried, as if reading from
the dictionary. Salvador
kept singing and we offered
the immigrants leftover
salad and what little
ham remained. "It was better
before we were barbarians,"
Franny whispered.
But they'd given us the wine
and wrapped it in wood,
and sent us a hollow horse
to hold our dreams in case
our hearts, at last, were full.

RIPPLES: I enter the daylight

like a vampire
to suck the last drop of the dew
on the green grass of August.

I enter the sounds scratching
the silences of this room.
In a corner, I see my grandfather
drinking tea for breakfast
in the old country.

Robust, with no fears,
he runs back and forth,
kneading a soft
loaf of bread with his hands.

Through the window, sun
defiantly
full of gossip, washes the city.
He walks to the door, leaving behind
the key to a *mandala*.

He is the heart of a
little girl waiting for his return. He is
the soft flapping in my ears.

Mariela Griffor

Chiloe Island

As night takes the capital of Santiago,
a thin crucifix hangs above the headboard.
A garden in the blankets' embroidery
embraced simple *copihues* and violets
and when we glance at these threads
they blink at us.
Who has the time to embroider tiny blue, yellow, red
flowers around the border of the quilt?
An old woman who knows the resilient
shape of the heart of a young woman
asleep for the first time with her husband.
No evil hand makes such a garden.
And when he came back to the hotel after his
lens in photography class saw everything
we ran up the street to a restaurant.
The smell of *curantos* and fresh bread
or corn pie, shellfish, and fishermen with red cheeks,
knives in harsh hands
that open that traitor, Pacific Ocean.
Ocean eats bodies in silence,
 succulent waters
spit up oysters or fish.

Back to the room, he calls me to warm his body.
We asleep as two old friends.
He asks if we ever had
a child and if he was not there I would leave the country.
Yes. I slept like a cat until morning.

The noisy street opens
 as I, going for my breakfast see
everyone going for lunch.
He wants me to pose with a lobster.
I agreed only if it's the last time
I touch shellfish. The last time.
We sit at the bus station he
whispers: we will be back on the island,
with the smell of shellfish, and noises of the sea
I would like that I told him. I saw
how walking under the water I return to Chiloe in secret:

stay long enough on the island
of corn pie, shellfish, and fishermen with red cheeks,
knives in harsh hands

that open that traitor, Pacific Ocean.
Ocean eats bodies in silence
 of those who dream on the island of Chiloe.

Mariela Griffor

The tale of two uncles

I grew up seeing his pictures everywhere in the house.
After the coup d'etat we hid his pictures in drawers
as you do with those uncles you need to hide
for whatever reason.
Everything changed. The most
profound and the most simple. I didn't
die as I used to think if I didn't live in
Santiago. The sun used
to rise between the mountains and the certainty
that when the sun was right behind
the tallest tip of the mountains facing the
city was the time to go to school. I didn't need
a watch to know the time. At evening when
I went back home a dusky red
entered my pupils and produced a fast pace to
my heart every time. Santiago was a dirty city
with pollution year round, full
of danger and poverty, excitement and wealth,
two small worlds for too many people.
Allende wanted to do something about it.
Uncle Sam didn't allow it.

from Preverbs

Defining Gesture

1
I promise you a rose garden. Now can we have dinner?

Let each thing be until its own extinction in fullness.
Until then give way to the originary middle voicing itself.

Not born again, made *over*, that decomposed recompose.
Wild field rose in full-fledged subjunctive — feathers flying!

2
If the line were not alive would it be talking to you like this?
Near messages may be hyperlocal rhetorics.

Remember, every dirty little secret hides a line of its own.
Even bad jokes enjoy a claim on reality.

You call wit what I witness calling.

Verbal dry fall, what once flowed, circling the hole in thought.
The wisdom impulse holds a dark cry concealed in flame.

George Quasha

3
Blank underline from unknown time — true home of what knows you?
I hear things.

Just as you think the force is spent it double-dares you.

Soon the living may find a way out through a sliver of line.

Not forward, yet all around throughout.
A constant circular movement around a mentally unseizable point.

Al-hayrah! — onto-onomatopoeic shakeout, hyperlocal being loose.
Ambiguity annoys unto the very root.

4
What can say *all* that's still denied?
This hunt for defining gesture hints the *stroke ending all doubt.*

Line, circumstance — going straight in bounding the empty.
Sign on the ledge: *slight alteration in signal wakes across.*

Stand still when you smile at meaning waving your quill.
Wonder further!

Discovery makes us — reach out lip first.
The legible edge strips bare....

GEORGE QUASHA

Configuring Principle

Part One
Inside the Theater of More (ToM)

I

You enter the place called *theater* or *playhouse* to see the play; you find your place there; then the play takes place. You yourself also come here to play, at least in your own mind, knowing that the play also takes place *inside you*. What's *out there* is also *in here*. Secretly, you *are* the theater, the playhouse, the place of the play, where your own life may seem to be staged right before your eyes; and here, under cover of private hiddenness, it gives up its secrets — if you have eyes to see. Your seeing eyes see both ways at once, the outer stage and the mirror stage within, the in/out threshold, the (double) ocular axis upon which your inner play plays out — the *thea* (Gk.), the view and the viewing that you, *theates* (Gk.), viewer, behold in the place of viewing: the theater. It's all you — well, it's also all the world.

And it's all me, and all not. We double, we straddle the threshold, confuse identities, we arc in the *viewing* between viewer and viewed, we spectators co-configure — we make theater side-by-side, each with our own play running privately inside. What renders this spectacle so spectacularly possible? Somewhere in here there is a *root principle* difficult to define and resistant to names, and yet it *has language*. Is it knowable? — and, if it is, in what sense is it known? And can we tell each other about it?

The hinge here is language: the principle that *has* language and can speak itself also *is* language. That's the starting point in this inquiry into principle; the realization that *a principle shows itself in the language by which it is thought.* It has what might be called a *poetics.*

Theater, to begin at the declared beginning of the *Theater of More,* is a word that carries a complex set of relationships, as indicated in its *viewer/viewing/viewed* etymology. A formulation like Giulio Camillo's 16th century *Theatro della Memoria* (1530) inherits a complex of traditions that play out the possibilities of viewing. This confluence of traditions includes the external site and architecture of the physical theater; the ancient mnemonic systems (*ars memorativa* as mnemotechnics) that combine primarily rhetorical systems with architectural images and nomenclature; the variously developed abstracted ancient rhetorical uses of mnemonics (Cicero, Quintilian); and the Hermetic tradition (Lull, Ficino) and magical and cabalistic practices able to incorporate mnemonic systematics in an esoteric agenda. The idea of *theater* in this broad history involves a range of meanings from the most external viewing to the deepest internal visionary experience. The word itself comprises, as it were, a kind of continuum running between the "outer" and "inner" meanings, and as such it is a threshold (*limen*) and site of liminality between extremes; and here a Camillo can play out his drama of mind-theater, its staged levels of "intellect" and "intention," ranging from the practical to the divine, with magical aspirations always ready to lift the next curtain.

Memory/Memoria too is such a *logoic* threshold.[1] I view *memory,* like *theater,* as what I call a *limen,* a liminal (non-)point of processual distinction within a continuum: on one hand, memory as

---

1 This quasi-coinage aims to neutralize a root term for "word" and "language," not to further valorize it, but to render it performative as a site of transitioning awareness/awareness transitioning, a certain thinking process.

rhetorical recall or as recollection (information retrieval) of facts, ideas, and rational formulations; and, on the other hand, memory as a site of restoration of powers, a return to fundamentals of one's intrinsic nature, an initiation that is both a discovery and an uncovering. "Theater of Memory" in the latter sense would be a site of what gets called magical, initiatic, and transformative experience, as indeed we may understand Camillo to have intended: *you go in as you and you come out as other.*

And in that sense there may be many subtle inheritors of such a "theatrical" tradition, perhaps including, say, Alfred Jarry's 'Pataphysics, Antonin Artaud's Theater of Cruelty (*Le Théâtre et son Double*), Jerzy Grotowski's "Objective Drama" and "Art as Vehicle," along with those connected to the latter (Peter Brook, Richard Schechner), and many more. Indeed, one could see certain performance artists here (e.g., Joseph Beuys, John Cage, Eiko and Koma, Marina Abramovic, Carolee Schneemann), and the list grows long as we locate the performative art that shares an initiatic/transformative principle somehow akin to that behind the Theater of Memory — art that fundamentally alters the participant. This performative art, of course, is not only *performance* art, but any art that embodies in its very structure and mode of operation such a *non-ordinary experience principle* — an initiatic unfolding that takes place in the inner theater of the participant.[2] One

---

2 Practically the archetype of the mind-changing performative structure is William Blake's *Jerusalem: The Emanation of the Giant Albion* (1802). And then there's *Finnegans Wake*.... If one expanded the focus in the contemporary, one could think of the music too of Morton Feldman, Terry Riley, La Monte Young, Pauline Oliveros, Franz Kamin, etc.; or the poetry of Charles Olson, Robert Duncan, Jack Spicer, Jackson Mac Low, Gerrit Lansing, Kenneth Irby, Robert Kelly, Charles Stein, etc. (But one would want to start not only with Blake but Goethe! Or James Joyce and Gertrude Stein!) Or the film art of Stan Brakhage and Harry Smith.... Yet the impulse here is not curatorial or anthological, but performative in the elucidation of a possibility in principle.

might think of Marcel Proust in this context, his discovery/recovery of a "lost" paradisal time-world through "involuntary memory" (via the petite madeleine) — this is something powerful, stunning, even life-changing, yet ultimately it is *ordinary* memory flying high. And then subsequently there is his discovery, formulation, and practice of "voluntary memory" — something entirely different—a principle of intentional world-(re)creation that is anything but ordinary. It conducts its magical mystery tour, young Marcel's "Magic Lantern" fully lit, and searches out lost time only to transport us far beyond the temporal, travelers in visionary syntax.

Yet "memory," Proust notwithstanding, no longer carries well the esoterically performative end of that logoic continuum, and the literalized word *memory* is cut off from its excitable liminality (except in coded usage, e.g., G.I. Gurdjieff's "self-remembering"). Such reasoning may have contributed to Heinrich Nicolaus'* name for his collaborative/participatory project, the *Theater of More* (ToM), resonating as it does with Theater of Memory yet avoiding tendentious or otherwise limiting associations that might compromise free participation. Given that it sets itself apart in this way, using a word (*More*) so broad and common as to seem adrift amongst undelimited reference, what might be its operative principle? The question is partly rhetorical; that is, if *thinking* its emergence in this way is already to *engage* it. The principle is active right here.

---

* Heinrich Nicolaus' ToM: Theater of More was a White Box (Bowery, NYC) exhibition (June 17–September 13, 2009), curated by Juan Puntes in collaboration with Wolf Guenter Thiel, focused on public dialogue and collaboration with a range of local and international artists, architects, musicians, film and video makers, new media artists, writers, actors, fashionistas, magicians, etc. Nicolaus also highlights the ideas of experts on Renaissance Art and Theory, including Max Seidel, Silvana Seidel Menchi and Gabrielle Perretta, and incorporates historical information furnished by archaeologist, Lucia Donnini, and architect Francis Levine who reference and postulate a time when art provided for and explored undifferentiated notions of science, spirituality, and

II
Execution is the Chariot of Genius.
— William Blake

Thinking in this sense, as engagement and performativity of principle, is inseparable from the language that embodies it. We can hardly think about our thoughts or examine them without scrutinizing the thinking language itself. Language reflecting upon itself! Chastened as we are by Wittgenstein to not be fundamentalists of language — those who believe in words as fixed realities with consistent referents (except by strict consensus or assigned meaning, as in jargon or code, with delimited application) — we labor to participate our thinking language *in process* and with *processual reflection*. This is where the poetics comes in, the working principles active in any given discourse. And further, the *thinking principles*, toward what can only be called a *poetics of thinking*.

We can look at the words engaged in thinking language, for instance, as sites of energetic charge. They have *history* (including both etymology and known historical uses) and *context*, as we have noticed above in the case of *theater* and *memory*. We noticed that each of those words can be viewed as a continuum between extremes of meaning. Therefore they are sites of more or less continuous transition. And they are thresholds, what I have called *limens*, logoic zones of liminality. If we examine any given moment

---

magic. Inspired by Giulio Camillo's Il Teatro della Memoria created in 1530, the multidisciplinary collaborative theater piece ("21") depicts processes and events of the present world crisis related to the imbalance between the soul and the world (anima mundi) as a backdrop for a multitude of new and inspiring actions and endeavors. Nicolaus reflects to some extent upon the influential communal attitude found in Paul Thek's collaborative artworks produced in the Low Countries during his exiled European years following completion of his critical work *The Tomb-Death of a Hippie*.

of thinking language, we may notice ourselves leaning to one side or another at the verge of distinction. In the example already examined, *theater*, I may be inside an actual theater looking at the stage, seeing the play as objective performance before me and yet feeling the emotional impact in a connection with personal experience, and I may even see this as *my* reality show playing itself out, while never losing track of the play *out there* as somebody else's work. There may be many levels of this back-and-forth focus, one level no more difficult than walking and chewing gum at the same time, another level many-tiered with wider and wider circles of referential engagement, and then a reflective level, much like the thinking we are doing here, and then: what? A certain leap, a non-ordinary giant step, a break in the frame, shadows with no projective light, figurings and unnamables — *the apparition of these faces in the crowd: petals on a wet, black bough.*

I resorted to poetry there, Ezra Pound's celebrated "In a Station of the Metro" with its visionary moment in the underground, catching the memorable light of certain faces in the flashing dark, calling back, in "an instant of time," lost souls from the underworld, Homer's Nekuia, *The Odyssey*, Book XI, happening again in the mind, the dark inner theater that at the far end crosses into death. It only takes one such experience, actually and powerfully realized, to transform a word for us — to make it a site again of a living continuum. To make it the *more* that opens us to a further knowing of our own being — and that, as we then can think it, is an instance of *real theater*. Theater thinking, as it were.

III

For this moment in thinking language we can go so far as to say that the principle of the *Theater of More* is a certain *theater thinking*. It's a space in which a lot of different kinds of things happen over time with no particular commonality of theme or point of view or artistic style or form or historical claim or political position or scientific pretension or concept of archival completeness or universality or system of information retrieval... you name it, it's not there, except as *more*. It lacks predictability. It makes for thinking. Thinking with a built-in *viewing space* in which many *viewers* focus on a certain *view*, here, now, in and of this moment. How? By way of an Art of More.

> *Reason, or the ratio of all we have already known,*
> *is not the same that it shall be when we know more.*
> — William Blake

More is an interesting word. It's practically the same in many languages — *ma* (Old English), *mo* (Middle English), *mehr* (German), *mas* (Spanish), *mor* (Old Irish) –*moros* (Greek), *mazja* (Avestan), and so on. No one can over-define it because all we can say is that what we have, so far, is less than it. Whatever we think about it is less than it already is by the time we say it, because it's *more*. The mind rushes ahead *toward* it. Thought is dislodged by it. Yet in that respect it's really like every word we use, because when we use it it's now more than it was; it now means *this*, yet just as this *is*, just now! — and quite clearly an instant later what we have said is already less than it. This is a pretty knotty affair, but have patience, it's telling us a lot about language.

Language is always being more as we use it, and it quickly leaves itself behind. It logo-degrades. Like thought. Like life. It hardly exists at all because, focused on *now*, it's confined to the no-space between less and more. The very thought of it calls into question the nature—nay, the very existence—of time, the present, an instant, the thought itself, as though, at the very threshold of *more*, there's hardly room for anything to *be* in time. Everything seems to be slipping out of time here, in this moment, in this theater of thinking more.

Perhaps this is the principle of the Theater of More: *theater thinking at the threshold of time and no-time.* After all, the language of *thinking it* keeps pulling the mind back to this spaceless space in which everything is potentially memorialized and nothing is retained—because it happens at the edge of being more. Memory must inevitably record what is not yet complete, what already knows it must be more. So, where is this theater and how do we remember where we are? You come in as yourself and you leave as other. As more.

It's as though the promise of more attracts thinking language to an unknown and unsayable further nature.

IV

Let's go back — well, that's not quite the right formulation at this juncture — let's go *on* with the way language itself is guiding us in configuring a principle of the present theatrical impulse. We are committed here in this joint enterprise to honor, to give priority to, the logoic entity (OK, the name) that has attracted us to this spot: *Theater of More*. We have been tracking its play. The transition from *memory* to *more* —

me**mor**ye

— a turn upon an invisible axis in language and thinking. You could say that there's a hidden space between *memory* and *more*. Turn the mind to the left and memory elucidates a world gone by — *more* now of what has been, remembered in a given moment. Turn the mind to the right and we're in the domain of what is only now dawning—recalling, at long last, what, now and now alone, can be *further*. This is what I call the *axis*, and the *axial moment*[3] — a moment, yes, but one with a curious *zero point* momentum, a force not quite, or not entirely, *in* time — or, rather, a force out of undertime. ...*the apparition of these faces*...

---

3 Axis can be thought of on many levels, from the intimate scale of the body and its spine, to the way physical things line up or pile up vertically, to the grand scale of the earth turning on its axis and its physical and magnetic polarities: how bodies *are* in space over time. Issues come up immediately—of balance, alignment, gravity, stability, precariousness, danger.... The axis, in most instances, is not primarily a *thing*, if at all, but a way of understanding physical events (earth turning, upright body walking), a concept, and indeed a principle of dynamic orientation of a body amidst physical forces. We use the word "axial" at times to engage the sense of personal relationship to the presumed or observed existence of an axis, and the potential for relative "freedom" in movement.

Well, anything can happen at zero point (which, of course, is not a "point"). There's zero predictability. There are zero limitations — there's nothing there! — it's between.

Perhaps only the Japanese have created a place in language for the thinking that wants to happen here in the between. In Kunio Komparu's great work, *The Noh Theater: Principles and Perspectives*,[4] a chapter is devoted to *ma* in which the range of meanings (from architecture to music) plays out as fundamental to the whole quite ancient phenomenon of Noh.

> As an expression of space, *ma* can mean space itself, the dimension of a space, or the space between two things....
>
> As an expression of time, *ma* can mean time itself, the interval between two events, rhythm, or timing....

This variability, or what I prefer to call *axiality*, suggests that in the case of *ma*, a long-standing usage recognized that the polarity of space and time is "polar" in a very special sense. Space and time are at once separated and linked by a pole in the sense of axis, a common hinge on which they swivel into "normal" appearance, now as space, now as time, depending on the perspective—and, in a sudden anomalous moment, as space-time. Physics, broadly speaking, produces this anomaly in mainly cognitive/conceptual and abstract terms, whereas art (Noh, as Komparu's analysis suggests) presents it sensorialy/intuitively and concretely. And *this* polarity, no doubt, has a hidden axis as well, a swing point within *ma* viewed as *principle*, suggested by Komparu's architecturally focused distinction in the subtitle, "*Ma*: The Science of Time and Space." The science in the

---

4 New York: Weatherhill/Tankosha, 1983, pp. 70-95.

art becomes indicator of an art dimension of science—a liminality function at the level of *ma* as principle, which shows up in the dynamic marriage of science (as theory *or* technology) and art, and, indeed, a certain indifference to the very distinction.[5]

So, perhaps this is the (or a) principle of the Theater of More: liminal theater, a theater of between, *ma*.

---

[5] Komparu himself was first a Noh actor in a long family lineage, who unexpectedly turned to writing as architectural critic, and just as unexpectedly returned in time to the Noh theater as actor. As one who crossed and recrossed a threshold between apparently incompatible disciplines, he was well-positioned to expose an infamous liminality within architecture itself in its science/art polarity — often, indeed, a struggle. He does this in part by focusing on the profoundly architectural aspects of Noh.

V

The true original is always yet to come.
— Ontononymous the Particular

Theater, for all its *seeing* and *being seen,* is also a place with a memory of speaking — and being heard. From ancient times it created a sense of *person* by way of masks and "speaking through" (*personando*) and of moving bodies and patterning energy. Language holds the center as the very possibility of *saying*, not necessarily, of course, with words, but also with movement, gesture, sound—and, at least since Artaud, theater has remembered itself as a language of *more* than words. Gesture can speak as unambiguously *or* as ambiguously as words, and the meaning-continuum of sound and gesture is as intensive *and* extensive as words, semantics, syntax, rhetoric. Its memory theater resides now, and primordially, in all that embodied being *says* itself to be, and in all the ways it now knows how. Its Art of More is a threshold of possibility. It is inherently innovative, although a self-image as avant-garde is a cultural artifact and not a sign of essence or relevance; nor is its value at issue in whether or not it's "been done before." Self-true language that speaks for itself is best understood as intrinsically *happening before,* and as inherently *unexampled.* (No polemic or self-consciously crafted identity as "new" will lend it extra primordial thrust.) The artifactual mask is ever a site of speaking through. One could point to its poetic principle as

living language speaks for itself

And it hones itself not by technique or technology, but simply by remembering its singularity — by focusing, that is, inside its own axis. Its "craft" is a function of attention and intensity in the process of self-unveiling — a stripping bare (bride or not) of self that's not particularly personal as such, yet stands true in the persona that *is sounding*. A happening in the space of an Art of More. A further theatricality that sees for itself.

Here we come upon the persona as *impersona*, a theater-entity whose very presence serves as a site of theater thinking — a sounded being, born in performance, a sort of *play birth*, a birth at play, and within *the play*. A projective entity. (Is there Golem poetics?) This species of performatively embodied thinking language is drawn out in the perspective of *more* — it's called out, so to speak, at the threshold of possibility, the lure of being, the irrepressible Pygmalion force, the eros of what can't bear *not existing*. And it allows us to focus on a sense of *co-performativity* and, paradoxical as it seems, a *poetics of shared singularity*.

Part Two
The Principle of Principle Art

We've been saying a lot about principle, without ever having defined it. The reason is simple, so simple in fact that it eludes understanding for more than a moment or so at a time. A principle can never be defined definitively, because any given definition is itself only a manifestation of the principle itself, appearing to be outside it. But principle has no outside, and in this way it's rather like a Klein Bottle, a continuous one-surface reality that morphs as it goes. Indeed we only see its morphs, just as you never see *the force that through the green fuse drives the flower*. It also invisibly drives Dylan Thomas' poem, which is in part its message, so structured, yet you *do* see the poem, or rather the words. There will be another, similarly visible and invisible, even if it should disavow it, saying things like *after the first death there is no other*: we know it lies to say what cannot be said, but must. That's how it works its principle of *more*.

There is obviously, in any given instance, a poetics of saying what we know to be there but can never point to directly. This is the whole problem of "higher" or "ultimate" or "fundamental" matters. It's no good to try to avoid it, which at best is only a more palatable or perhaps sophisticated game of charades. Nothing is solved by avoidance. Principle is here to stay.

I have taken a stab or two at it where not to say *something* only adds to confusion:

> Provisionally I would say principle is the basic or essential element determining the *evident functioning* of particular natural phenomena, mechanical processes, or art emergence.

Yet it's as much a *force* as an "element," depending on the context. And a view of it does depend on context, which gives it a skin, an outside. But scratch that surface and it disappears. For principle is not so much a one-surface as a *no*-surface reality — until it *surfaces*. Mostly it shows up looking like a concept. If it can't be firmly identified, how can an artist use it and remain true to it? The answer: the artist's art knows how.

The first opportunity to make some distinctions is to look at it art-historically, where in fact an understanding of principle-based art (which has apparently never called itself that, at least until now) can clear up some misunderstandings and reveal certain priorities that are rarely foregrounded. Once better understood, certain artists and their approaches may attract more accurate attention. However, this is unlikely to happen until we grasp better how principle (and, indeed, the principle of principle) works in the case of particular artists.[6]

There is an obstacle in the complexity of the phenomenon of *conceptual art*, which of course takes many paths and, at this late date, has so integrated into a wide range of art practices that, except in the much discussed "classic" instances, it can hardly be distinguished as a separate phenomenon in contemporary art. This is not the place to address this complexity except in the broadest terms, focusing on a common denominator of much conceptual art for the purpose of distinguishing it from what I call *principle art*.

---

6 In collaboration with Charles Stein, I have taken steps in this direction in *An Art of Limina: Gary Hill's Works and Writings*, Foreword by Lynne Cooke (Barcelona: Ediciones Polígrafa, 2009). I have also written about it reflectively in relation to my own art practice: *Axial Stones: An Art of Precarious Balance*, Foreword by Carter Ratcliff (Berkeley: North Atlantic Books, 2009).

Axial, liminal, configurative:[7] These three terms comprise both a complex *principle*, as we see it in its tripartite appearance, and a possible (but not necessary) sequence in the interrelated way that the principle unfolds in experience. They also embody three ultimately inseparable aspects of a commitment to principle in art. Principle in this particular usage differs from "concept" and "conceptual" but is in no way opposed to them. An artist working from principle in this sense may also be working with concept, but they are not interchangeable terms. Of course, as the history of art particularly since the 1960s has shown, there is a range of possible ways of defining and using "concept" and "conceptual." Yet we can notice in a number of cases that a concept is definitively represented by the work that it produces; indeed, one kind of conceptual "ideal" might be: one concept, one work. A principle, in contrast, cannot be fully defined by the work it produces or inspires or operates within. A principle can be endlessly renewed through well-defined yet non-definitive manifestations, and an endless variety of works can be produced out of it. Paradoxically a principle is not often well served by apparent repetition (unless the principle calls for it); a true manifestation of principle, the way I mean it here, is a singularity.[8]

The principle of a principle-based work is not necessarily *prior* to, as "leading up to," the practice. Though a given principle in some sense had to already be there before the practice began, the decisive point is the artist's discovery or direct awareness of it, which

---

7   This section is adapted from the Prologue to *An Art of Limina* (previous note). I have not attempted here a full exposition of the tripartite principle.

8   Fluxus artist Dick Higgins once created a neat conceptual work in a button with the words, "If you can't do it twice you haven't done it." A reverse concept would better represent principle: "If you can do it twice you still haven't done it."

may or may not function as *motivation* for making the work. This would be a key distinction between *principle-based* art and *conceptual* art: the latter would seem by definition to be substantially in place prior to execution of the work. Work grounded in principle, by contrast, is neutral on this issue. A given work may have a strong conceptual focus at the beginning or not; but this basic fact—that it *can* be subject to processual evolution through open composition—alters the status of even its conceptual strategies. The root principle is open. In this regard, for instance, Gary Hill has said of early, foundational work: "…the space that I often attempt to work in…[has made it possible for] many of the single-channel works [to be] structured in such a way as to allow… unpremeditated activity on my part in producing them." And, discussing installation work like *Tall Ships* (1992):

> My working methodology is not one of theorizing and then applying that to making art. In each work I find myself committed to a process that of course may involve material where… philosophical issues may seem to be relevant. But I'm committed to the idea that the art event takes place within the process. One has to be open to that event and be able to kind of wander in it and feel it open up; to see it through until some kind of release feels inevitable.[9]

This basic attitude may be seen as comparable to the approach of certain older artists who were working during his early development, say, Stan Brakhage in film; John Cage, La Monte Young, or Terry Riley in music; Charles Olson, Robert Duncan, Jack Spicer, Jackson Mac Low, Allen Ginsberg, Robert Kelly, or David Antin in

---

9 Regina Cornwell, "Gary Hill: An Interview," *Art Monthly* (October 1993); reprinted in *Gary Hill*, edited by Robert C. Morgan (Baltimore: A PAJ Book, The Johns Hopkins University Press, 2000), p. 224ff.

poetry; or, of course, the "action painting" of the 1950s and 1960s, as well as a good deal of body and performance art (Yoko Ono, Carolee Schneemann, Vito Acconci) from the 1960s on. Yet in matters of art principle it is not of primary interest to think by way of comparison or the idea of influence or the claim of priority, except incidentally, or as a way of being in touch with historically resonant event fields. An artist working from a matrix of free action and according to an emerging vision certainly *feeds* on art and thought, but that means many *kinds* of art and thinking, beyond all anticipation.

The work itself as *limen*

The challenge of developing a practical criticism that reveals principle at work in certain artists is no simple matter, especially since consistency and repetition are *not* particularly virtuous in principle-based work. Yet we can take a small step in that direction here by way of an installation work by Gary Hill.

Coming to terms with terms: The noun *limen*, threshold, has the meaning of *smallest detectable sensation*, the *unit* of what crosses the line. In physiology, psychology, or psychophysics, a limen or liminal (non-)point is a threshold of a physiological or psychological response. In this technical context, *liminal* means *situated at a sensory threshold*, hence barely perceptible. A limen is therefore close to *vanishing point*. This helps us understand the academic and social domains in which the concept of liminality has played a significant role, such as psychology, as noted, but also more loosely in the description "liminal personality" for someone "near the edge (or breaking point)." And in the social sciences, notably in anthropology, there is the work of Victor Turner, who has written influentially of its implications for social status, saying, for instance: "Liminal entities are neither here nor there; they are betwixt and between the positions assigned and arrayed by law, custom, convention, and ceremonial."[10] In a sense, a liminal person is "barely perceptible" and living at the social "vanishing point."

In the 1996 installation *Viewer*, Gary Hill projects the life-size images of seventeen marginalized men (mostly Latino, Native American, and Black dayworkers) who obviously live near the social vanishing point. The men, somewhat as if in a police lineup, stand a bit uncomfortably facing out at viewers. When we view them seemingly viewing us, their sad and vacant eyes gazing into our art-inquiring eyes, we enter into their liminality—and perhaps discover some portion of our own. The art space, itself a liminal zone (the outer banks of society at large), is *further liminalized* by virtue of our reflective empathy. We might say that we engage *marginal viewing*: There's our viewing their marginal status and their viewing back from the margin. At another level, perhaps there's our awakened self-view as belonging to the social class (gallery, museum, art market) that unfortunately contributes, however unintentionally, to their marginalization; and, quite possibly, the momentary *reversal* of that in our opening our eyes to *them*. Maybe also

---

10 Our sense of "liminality" was worked out independently of its usage in anthropology, which, while different in focus, is not incompatible with ours. Victor Turner took the term from Arnold van Gennep's threefold structure of ritual in *The Rites of Passage* (1909, 1960), and developed it in *The Ritual Process: Structure and Anti-structure* (1969) and subsequent works. In the essay "Liminality and Communitas," Turner notes: "Prophets and artists tend to be liminal and marginal people, 'edgemen,' who strive with a passionate sincerity to rid themselves of the clichés associated with status incumbency and role-playing and enter into vital relations with other men in fact or imagination. In their productions we may catch glimpses of that unused evolutionary potential in mankind which has not yet been externalized or fixed in structure."

there's our honest awareness that, only here in this liminal (but safe) space of art (as opposed to actually standing in front of them on a street corner), do we get to be *this* kind of viewer, in all its resonance. In this very moment, standing as we are at the threshold of self-awareness, the *viewing* is the limen, the barely appearing crossing point into newly reflective awareness. And the work, *Viewer*, is itself the limen—the actual threshold—that makes all this happen.

In general, as well as in most of the specific ways that we have referred to it, *liminality* is a concept, a cognitive frame within which we understand, or apperceive, various relationships of center (self/entity) and periphery (other/world). It also stands for, indeed *signals*, the *act of framing* that allows us to mentally stand back and reflect upon an open state of objectifying—to grasp, for instance, that some objects are non-ordinary and demand special attention, perhaps even new orders of attention—*singular acts of attending*. We can recognize *liminal objects* without really knowing what they are. We grant them, at least provisionally, an honored status. And we find ourselves in dialogue with othernesses, states of oscillatory engagement with unnamables—and maybe it makes us want to speak out, even out loud, and talk with unknown things, alien objects. At a certain point in this process, such as when we realize that the object before us, the *work* or *opus*, is itself a liminality, a limen, a unitary agent of some kind of energetic exchange at an edge, or transformative or transportive event, or indeed *synergy*. At that point *liminality as concept* has become *liminality as principle*. The merely *thinkable* has become a unique kind of *doable*, an event at large, something happening with perhaps unclear agency. And once we see this we can give up trying to know what it is in advance of experiencing its actual instance. Singularity is possible.

The point of laying out this notion of the work itself as limen, its embodiment of liminality at the level of principle, is to signal a shift in view. In a sense, a work that functions as limen—as vehicle of liminalizing our very state of participation—is already a further threshold, a crossing point to a unique state that cannot have been before its (this) very moment. We may be even be arriving here at a threshold of "social sculpture." This would be an aspect of the shifted, and shifting, view. The work is always a further instance of itself—which is why it is open, completely incomplete, *able*, that is, to be incomplete through the fact of interminable completeness. The work is "living" in the sense that it is self-regenerating and non-repeating.

We may see our role here, not as "art criticism/history," but *functional* within the historical stream of art. In that sense it is what we have often called the *further life of the work*. The object we are discussing is changing as we speak, even *in* what we are saying. And how do we convey that status but by taking responsibility for it? Further life comes through co-performance, for which there is a critical discipline: it arises from within the work itself, peculiar to responsibility understood as precise responsiveness. Or as the poet Robert Duncan put it: "Responsibility is keeping the ability to respond."

The resonance of principle art is felt in the thinking it inspires — thinking that *furthers* its realization. This excursion into a resonant field tracks the inauguration of a project — Theater of More — to explore its alignment with a practice of *principle thinking*. That thinking, in search of a possible poetics therein, is always turning and situating itself within its axis, always playing itself out at the edge, and always configuring itself and the reality before it. This brings us to the beginning of the inquiry.

Brian Henry

Closet Theater

Shroud, veil, thread.
Soggy ball of yarn.
Baptise the package, and drown.

Food Court

An hour burnished
as if time could bear
a sheen.

Brian Henry

Snuff Film

There is no
bird here
going peep.

Mescal's Wager

Down
in case of
absence.

K.A. Thayer

Curtis Byvarsky

Curtis Byvarsky swallowed a mirror, whereupon it recreated all of its reflections. In the belly of Curtis Byvarsky there lies digesting a story of another world, now broken into a language of bloody shards too hard to speak with just two rows of plain teeth.

K.A. Thayer

The Garden Variety Pneumatic Pigeon

This bloodbath, no, sorry, birdbath of innertubes attracts the occasional gymnast or prize fighter. They like the rebound but can't compete with the pigeons. In a pinch, trees get wrapped with inflatable rafts and mattresses. The pigeons have a high reputation, disguised as lawmakers and politicians. It's the garden of green thumbs. The sanctuary of sacking and somersaults. The unfortunate predicament arises when overfeeding occurs. Guano knee-deep, the trees exclaim their virtues: canopies of shelter, nest-keepers, weigh-anchors for crying lives of air-eaters, feather-droppers—strong-limbed noose-holders for necks snapped from excessive sadness—a desire to escape gravity — the strangling blow of ceaseless opponents.

K.A. Thayer

Escapade of The Unspoken

People look and listen.
I look at and listen to people.
They look at and listen to me.
I disappear.
They disappear.
The world disappears.
It's made of fine thread.
Inside the thread
is a loaf of bread
going stale.

Pigeons warble and peck,
gestures nearing speech.
As the wings of the plumpest one ruffle,
I open my former mouth.
Out comes Houdini
holding a lockpick,
disemboweled,
asking for stronger chains
and a crumb.

A sign left for those
who hope to re-appear.

Language about language its
dull that is dulling a dullant
still sweeping over the thing words
that try try not to be words that
do not say not trying to say that is
to blurt the thing they are saying
as in the hair was trapped under
the skin making that sore making the area
red but really sweeping away the non-thing
beneath that shame or silent unsayable I
have a body imperfect and pain and
trying to soothe it is just like that
language a still but sweeping dull but I try

Leah Souffrant

Heard the unspoken words – rain, car lights.
The flow of no hope *saw the dear face*. Turn
    away *so it is*. *Saw the dear face and heard
the unspoken words.* And we drink the cool

the pavement dances, moving when
    with earlier rain
    storm and passing car lights, when
the glow of the lamp above
    the mirror above the sink above
    the face turns warm, like pink,
when no hope of words remain I hear your
    eyes turning toward me and my neck
    saying my face must   turn away.
So it is 2 a.m.

Sleep walking. Slipping out of bed. Light of the refrigerator
illuminating
    the face, the legs. Water is too cool. Too cool.

Heard the unspoken words – rain, car lights.
The flow of no hope *saw the dear face*. Turn
    away *so it is*. *Saw the dear face and heard
    the unspoken words.* And we drink the cool
Water   We sleep we walk and turn, turn away We turn toward
    the unspoken words, the hope, cool
midnight. Turn away, turn still.

all that we are in holding

it was up to me
to put my arms around
her shoulders
gently crossing over
her heart

those were the days
when we danced
in the dark
with no music

she told me to never let go.

Sylva Boyadjian-Haddad

Triptych

I

Dioscuri

Monozygotic twins we could have stayed
if on that day the fog had lifted you
would not have gone down that road I the other

seabound now you swim the bottom
weightless I hover long shadow into ether
neither of us earthbound

your attempt to grab me — vain
mine at lifting you up mere gesture
mimicked endlessly

as it sinks and shimmers and evanesces
ripples making our movements figure eights
forever multiplied

always in unison a marvelous symmetry
of form never union — sharpened pencil point desire
never pinned down

II

Homage to Dionysus

Grace does come to the celebrant
from memory stored in limbs and
the rush of blood echoing in the ears
reverberating from soil to sole of feet
uniting dancer with a familiar beat

III

Inconsolable

Why still that ache near the heart
after renouncing desire
why the longing for the desert
why so wistful when silence falls
so close to stillness

World's Wild Fire

> Flesh fade, and mortal trash
> Fall to the residuary worm; world's wildfire, leave but ash
> Gerard Manley Hopkins

All night it raged in the distance, so when I
woke to see it at the window, I wondered
if the whole world was on fire: a long red wall
of flames consuming the valley until the trees
stood naked and burned like candles.
                              Then clear
at dawn, each day a genius at forgetting.
                              I rose
from the cellar where I had cowered listening to the fire
repeat its name and searched the clouds for the things
that had burned: trees, houses, fields, barns.
Watched their shapes turn to forms, then back
again in the otherwise blue, oblivious sky.

Chard deNiord

From Box to Box

For Rayna

"See how blurry you can make the trees.
See how high you can lift your knees."

"As long as the gerbils cling to the wheel…"

A blur on the track. A tree with a watch.

"At the sound of my stopping you will wake."

"Speak to me now in your stillness beneath the trees."

"The whole time I was running I was thinking
about something else, although I couldn't stop,
although the earth had become a wheel
and I was running to stay in the world.
I saw that I was running too far, that we
were growing farther apart the closer we got
on the track, that love wanders *from box to box.*"

Flying & Misleading Monikers

The bat—
the only mammal that flies—
    let dreams be.

The flying squirrel
in identity crisis—merely glides—

missing that
tree trunk
    (then doubly bilked).

—Don't picture Zaha Hadid—

concerned with fixed elements, movement and speed—

    (she, *the night ool* her Italian staffer says).

But back to the bat,
black, diaphanous from the ground, barely
    walks (did you know?) but hoists itself

  into the air —
    — its own power.

Talia Katowicz

Espressioni per la tavola

Fig. (1)
Ti posso offrire qualcosa da bere/mangiare?
May I offer you something to drink/eat?

Educated by Emilys: Post and Dickinson plot themselves into the kitchen with respective tools. One spreads a stunning table in shades of ecru and emerald while the other wears a white apron, pens a note on desire, and folds the linen napkins for you. If you prepare your world with proper etiquette, the prettiest guest gets served first. Would you like an hors d'oeuvre? Do you prefer red or white? Listen to the following dialogues and decide who will starve and who will be satisfied.

Fig. (2)
Perché no? Lo/La prendo/bevo volentieri.
Why not. I'll eat/drink it with pleasure.

Our grandmothers refuse the last dinner roll or puff pastry, even when they ache for something else. Our fathers take the first bite and declare it good before they've finished chewing. At dinner the plates are passed clockwise until the pattern on the serving bowl can be discerned: plume-spread peacocks, rose-of-sharon, arabesques like sleeping question marks. Residue of gravy or olive oil glitters. It will collect at the rim as all good intentions aim for empty, ask for just enough.

Fig. (3)
Non fare/faccia complimenti: ne prenda un altro po'.
Don't be shy: have some more.

What if, after the first miracle, there were no others? If we gathered the gall to ask, "do that wine skin thing again!" and our Lord merely sighed, thought of carpentry or a trip to the Cape. We scrape plates and squeeze memories with less shame, take what is offered when it is good; when it is gone we wonder. By farce or chance, hosts calculate indulgence, guess gluttony at all expense. The human condition prays He saved the best for last, eyes its neighbor's dish, counts peas, pleadingly.

Fig. (4)
Mi dà la ricetta?
Can you give me the recipe?

Your mother's Latin eyes and your father's nervous laugh and your brother's way of leaving and your sister's cleft chin and the awkward habits inherited from TV and workplace interaction and your favorite novel heroines and there must be something to evolution besides monkeys and mandates and the right measuring spoons and stirring vigorously and recognizing a rolling boil and buying only the best ingredients and indenting each paragraph and all pleasure is a riddle with the evening meal that can't be printed in a book or bought on sale or sold discretely with a packaged smile for the politeness of table companions, but, oh, this is really delicious.

Talia Katowicz

Ariadne

northern stars	My dowry was a clue of thread, a sword
white-hot blooms	to slay my brother, big bully with an
a wedding garland	a p p e t i t e for adolescents –
strung across the sky:	s e v e n p e r y e a r t o y o u r one,
corona borealis	you remember? I was too eager
this abandoned bride,	to please, T h e s e u s, sandal-bearer
cretan beauty *banished daughter*	Athenian. Before you came I braided
"i want to be adored"	the black hair of dolls, never uttered
awash on a beach	"I want to be your dog." Not out loud.

        Stars in my eyes, mere girl, without shame, but shivering, waiting by the labyrinth for you to appear. Blood on your hands, wishing you were clean. You kissed me by the harbor and, bewitched by foreign lips, I laughed while you bored holes in the bottoms of Minos' ships.

Tamara J. Madison

Solicitation

wanted:
dreamers, artists
to color the people;
no mockery,
no revisionist histories;
encouragement
to colour
outside
the lines.

Tamara J. Madison

Not Only a Tupac Poem

for every ebony manchild
catching bullet or blade
between teeth or spleen
with one wink of the sun
a star sheds its skin
instead of a tear
the slough slips   slithers
among the heavenly bodies
lilts on a wilting wind
wriggles through the whimpering leaves
of a willow
lands softly on a regiment
of weeds kneeling to bear it as honor
before it slips again
disintegrates as seeds
in sanguineous soil fecund with prophecy
titanium threads root
form silver stems ascending
veining concrete to crumble
as copper waters break   baptize
the crowning heads
of cast iron
roses…

Neighbor Trees

In the shade of a crab-apple,
I'd pretend to be an orphan,
forced to eat the bitter fruit.

I would have traded all
my paltry secrets for just one word
from the trees, for example, *Ailanthus*

dropping sticky tassels into our hair,
as we hopped over chalk squares
scribbled in the street.

They wouldn't have had to approve of me;
it's not a tree's place to pity.
Houseplants took care of that:

Elephant Ears nuzzling my hand
from a cracked green vase,
Prayer Plant, applauding
lobed leaves. I confused

myself with a Weeping Willow:
back bent, roots reaching deep
for water, knuckling through concrete.

ALICE B. FOGEL

Variation 29: Boats

                       Boat after boat after boat after boat
            hulls bottom up beside the hushed lake, cold

        abandoned boats, scaled notes up and down
along the staff of shore. Boat after boat after boat

         pulled up the slope, overturned, overarched
under the arc of sky. Crouched like soldiers,

           faces hidden, whelmed at the ground.
Prisoners of other wars: tethered, tree-tied,

            locked and chained: boat after boat
              bound to the hard dirt bank

      and left to splinter dry all winter long.
                   Sundown pasteling

the luminated lake, lake mirroring everything:
    Water's smooth proof of boat after boat.

      Shore boat / lake boat—dome / bowl—
    the shined flipside
                of the other hand:

Because down the long inclined
 far shore, beneath that wooden road

  of rowboats heavy, scattered side by side, light
   boat doubles float like lake's own remembrance

    of their dead weight once lofted easily
     like heroes on its back. More boats

      oppositely upside down,
       cupped, two wrongs making one right

        side up against the depth of water pressed
         to the sky. Below, birds flow, past trees and cloud

          fish nod. And reflected in the skimming
           light borrowed from a dimming sky: boat after boat after

            borrowed boat—borrowed by water, by land.
             Oh, boat, boat, spirit boat: That I might hover too

              on the battlefield of another shore,
               neither adrift nor drowned.

Alice B. Fogel

Variation 10: Moths

Long once, hung from oaks, dangled rungs of boneless
flesh webbed in open nets among branches, the green

edgy leaves rotten limp. Fantastic scourge of furred
black columns balanced from lanky cords spit

from our own dumbstruck mouths. O the life in the trees,
our weighted fringe slung over roofs and streets, that rapt

business of crawling in the sun, the great solidity!
Now our dank houses tight wound all down our sides —

all sides that we are — and what did we do to deserve this wrap
inside time out outside of time, hidden, as if repentant

and intent upon resurrection? Our only actuality anticipation,
so becoming to itself. What do you take us for?

All right, it's true, we're lying here stupid, duped.
So that after this, all at once one fine night, shaken

we can come to as little moths, cute
and foolish as flakes of summer snow and all for what —

we ask you. One slanting flurry of florid white wing
spilling, one feeble pulse of flight against the wrist

of one midnight: at dawn dismissed
to wisp and stillness, royal carpets of broken

wing flipped and swept across the expanse
and left to highlight every crack already veined

on roadways. Should we look forward to a flick
of life first as circle and cloud amassed

at streetlamps and then dropped, nearly done for,
a sweep of creeping outline, a brief and pallid grout

between the permanent stones? O we
once the sinewed, we the firm, we the chewing length

of leaf and stem squirm and warm, banned
to those slight cursive runes scrawled into crevices

and coiled along ditches like over-elongated reminiscences,
mere wan traces, of our darker former selves!

Louise Landes Levi

Mr. Bliss

I
always wanted to
thank Mr. Bliss

(an <u>ex</u>- funeral director)

for the $50.00 he gave me in

KK's

But

I
never saw
him
again

(not remembering clearly how he looked)

I'd ask the elderly clients
are you Mr. Bliss?

but they
never

were

NYC 1997
after Allen's death

Don't Be Scared

        Forsythia, Daffodils/
        Apple Pear blossoms/ green
    Grass, heavy rainfall, flirtation w. D.

        Glamour girl/ glitter girl/
            Hippie
                girl,

'Don't be Scared'/ yr. not alive – Why is M.
  falling for that same
                old
                        line?
    I miss her/

        drinking carrot juice

                            again/
        Issa
    waited his whole life for his patrimony
      then his father's house
          burned
            down

          *

NYC 2005

LOUISE LANDES LEVI

Blue Bird

                  Now
           that I turned
  into
         a Sanskrit letter & felt
       yr. heart in my heart on the
         corner of 106th street
                              &
                                         Broadway,

                Now
         that I dream of you
      as a giant blue-bird made

    by children, as I glance into a
  mirror & slip trees fr. my white as
     placing them w. care in a
      tin-can for umbrellas, O
                       lost
                               loves,

    Bathing together, flying even,
     I uncross my lotus legs
       & am released
            in
                     space.
            This
  morning's winter fire comforts
 as I search for you in roman cards
   & no one, not even I, can

READ
THE
FUTURE.
NYC 2004

Lana Hechtman Ayers

East Rockaway

after T.S. Eliot's East Coker

"I keep my ideals, because in spite of everything I still believe that
people are really good at heart."
—Anne Frank

"Home is where one starts from."
—T.S. Eliot, *East Coker*

I

Where I started is not where I'll end. A succession
of selves, pre-verbal, pre-school, then defined
by school, the early awkward digits, the gawky teens,
the ungainly college and young adult years constrained
by love, contained by new love, stained with lost love,
trained by lost love to gain new love, to maintain love
which is akin to restraining the earth from turning.
Flinting from humankind, young and older
love burns and burns out: there is a time for yearning
and a time for grieving, for solitude's blues
and a time for moonlight to slide between shut blinds
and for sunlight to rut chaste blood again
and for strutting in strumpet winds, passion renewed.

Where I started is not where I'll end. Now the sun rises
over the wild sea, illuming a thoroughfare
uncluttered by vessels, glittery in the early day,
where you loll on a sandy spot as a white gull wheels,

and the thoroughfare hails you to sail along it
toward light's windblown face, in cool dawn
enthralled. This high tide, there's low fetch,
the crests and swells are gentled.
Silver salmon swim in slackened sound.
The cormorant is close at hand.
                              Over that wild sea
if you keep your eyes wide, if you keep your ears tuned,
one summer morn, you will hark calypso music
piping playfully from prodigious speakers
and see gleeful revelers on the promenade
of a great contraption of a sailing vessel
borne for pleasure in paradise.
In what many would call undignified display
pairs and triads and odder configurations
hand in hand, arm in arm, grabbing one another
to dance the rhythms, round and round the deck.
Leaping past lifeboats, they form a conga line
with asynchronous high-kicks, boisterous laughter
clumsy hops and colliding stops
their sea lags new and wobbly, lifted in mirth.
Mirth in spite of those left behind on land
punching the clocks. Becoming free,
free in the rhythm in their dancing
living as they do not in their daily lives
free on the high sea under the wide sky
free to drink and dine to excess
free to couple and copulate
free as beasts. Finger snapping, toe tapping.
Feasting and frolicking. Hijinx and hangovers.

    Dusk comes, and another night
readies for secrets and sleep. Back on land dusk winds
blow in and in. I am here,
you there, or elsewhere. In our distant nows.

Cambodia: Sad Little Girls

Chanilla: "Nights with Her Father"
she wanted to scream
out, wanted to bite like
a wild animal
she was small,
he held her down like she
was made of gossamer
yet, she felt like her body
was full of tar

Hong, in a back room,
the fold of her outsides
sewn into the interior;
Born a little flower,
she will bleed on command.

Jorani's Dream
I wake in a bed made of
pink cotton candy—
jackfruit and coconut juice,
slices of mango, orchids in
bittersweet apricots,
fuchsias, and amethysts,
glittering so brightly that my
Mother can see
I send her a message—
through the luminous language
of the flowers, their colors variegated

like the girls imprisoned in the rooms
next to mine
You did not mean to
leave me with that woman
Come to me Mama—
Mama, wipe me clean

KATHLEEN FAGLEY

Sedna

Between Pluto and the Oort Cloud,
in the outer regions of the solar system,
a planetoid—discovered by accident

in Palomar's automated sweep of the sky.
Named for Inuit goddess of the sea,
you emerge from deep space

or what we thought was deep space.
Not quite a planet or Kuiper Belt object—
you swim in our purview, lazily,

scribing a wide orbit, ejected outward
from somewhere else. Eccentric
third cousin to our nine, you move in time

to another sun, unseen but felt.
If I stood on your surface,
the sun would be like moon; to the left,

hazy plane of our Milky Way.
Sagittarius would be closer,
Earth a stain on the sky.

Yet when I turn away from all I know
and look outward—trillions of bodies
reach from here to the next galaxy.

I believe in you, Sedna,
a word on the tip of my tongue,

faint pinpoint of light in my peripheral vision
gravitating to the next something else.

Suffer the Frogs

1
Come to me as you did
twenty years ago, in abundance:
a forest of frogs set in motion
by my steps. Polished green
jewels in the fog and mist,
the only color that day.

I broke through some cloud,
a lack of clarity.
A miracle I thought and still do.
Now my miracles are lean and few.

2
I learned you backwards—
by dissection.
Pale underbellies slit,
coiled intestine and eggs,
the size of infant tears.
Skin folded back like an envelope.
White human-like legs held in pincer grasp.
Frogs tossed, stuffed in boys' pockets,
thrown in girls' laps.
I felt you once in my open palm,
your body a muscle that leapt
into vanishing.

3
Gone from the hills of California,
cloud forests of Costa Rica.
Your porous skin—the chemical and poisons
you generously take in.
Cold-blooded amphibian,
you are misnamed.
I name you Oracle of the Setting Sun.

LEE ANN BROWN

But tenderly and with high math

> after Edna St. Vincent Millay

But tenderly and with high math
To hunger garments upon the church —
Northern children tune in unintended

Compressions unfold — Lesson Nine on
Planet Nine convert that energy
Cast about words — Unkempt

Mother's commands are spelled:
 "Eat" "Sleep" "Why?"
Trigger and tickle mortal infants —
Both spider and Fly —

Break up capital's habits

Mother says grow up and feel good this
Time — break your Yes bound
up in No — Chart — vibrating
Desire — DNA — "What do we want?"
To grow out of our Toys —
Angered by day — Drawn alchemy at night.

Lee Ann Brown

Ampule

Ampule's sketchy rule of thumb endeavored
to prepare the beds for our downfall

A lilac time is in the hall
Expanded out paint chipped in half light

Ampule's sketchy rule of thumb relevered

Doggy's purple stimulation undone —
                              "nothing's wanted"

Ampule's sketchy rule of thumb outlaws that plaid
Arrogance of ambidextrous forms, marvels at

The way we go out from our untrue selves

I get up and cross the room — obligated to project as a

Peony page flutters backs up the stair

Insightful intrepid
   figured into the
      green girl
         on my
            right

         Isabella

Fibrous optic quivering heat

    & kept up

    <We are>

   vines in the sun

Oleander
scribbles

My friend Linda
    would trace out the

handwritten voices
you're good at flowing by &

        in & over it already

    set it down
  in order others
      might live

out the Elegaic Mode

Cloisters —

On the way I laugh at the
   little boats
foundering on the

Hudson

Rhythms on the
   hill
  the old rugged cross
and wooden madonna with tear-filled eyes

The other side of the fabric is just as rough & smooth
     as its other —
Spinning the objects of desire — "Why Not?"
Maybe
We LIKE living in Three Dimensions
     rather than Four!
But if the 4th dimension
     is time
that would make sense

  We ARE rolling right along

Agency & intentionality are so essentialist!

If I rolled down this hill
I would be stung by Many Bees.

LAURA DAVIES FOLEY

"The Hands of Russia Are Long"

I wonder if the Polish ambassador tripped
in his ablutions, if he trembled as these words
spilled over him, slipped from Russian into
Polish tongue by Stefan Sharff, né Leon Lench,
translator, young consul general, who would soon
defect, change his name, and then, at sixty,
marry me, a student forty years his junior.

These words, that would mean death
for millions, exile to tens of millions,
dropped from Stalin's lips as he stood pissing
in the Moscow Hotel, words of threat
sutured over later, during a formal dinner
where few could eat.

Words that come down to me as history,
long hands of Russia, gripped in the urinal.

Janet Barry

Spring Cleaning

Rag-bones/Rag-bones
Dead-feather fluff in the mud —

The owls ate all winter,
But not enough — So Spring clean,

Turkey Vulture,
First on the scene —

Beat the rugs/Sweep and scrub
Beat the rugs/Sweep and scrub

We've had enough
Of our Rag-bones/Rag-bones
Dead-feather fluff — so Pick them clean,

Turkey Vulture,
First on the scene —

Scour and wring/Scour and wring

We've had enough
Of our dead-feather fluff —

And our filthy
Winter
Roadkill
Rag-bones.

Fossil Fuel

fossil imprint on rock
resting under Burgess Shale fern
stamps a moment when earth
hot inside, cold on surface, lives.

saber-toothed cats, giant sloths
heave bodies out of evolution
while tough green moss
under heavy snow
moves with creaking ice floes.

as melting begins, green blankets
warm hidden places, pricked into life
algae, worms, sea cucumbers work
millions of years to form a world.

like tiny trilobite in Cambrian stone
our bodies press against each other
print wet marks on the ancient rocks
easily washed away by sharp rain.

Tara Betts

Marin County, August 7, 1970

Brother of a Soledad Brother took over,
called William, James and Ruchell. They fled
with judge, lawyer and three jurors held
hostage. Each one thought of as shield
against jaws that crush their manhood — hard
dark candies, bitter as what they exposed
when the police fired. Even the judge died.

Kent State, 1970

Flowers are better than bullets, one student shout
before ROTC fell as ash and ember
while cheers rose like loud flames popping,
before guard hemmed with student jeers stood
trapped on Blanket Hill. So they claimed
after firing into unarmed throngs. Lights shine
where four souls have been parked forever.

Jackson State, 1970

No more hollers from Lynch Street, no
rumors shot down Charles Evers and wife,
no more Vietnam. No student knew how
13 seconds held over 400 shots. Each
bullet led grim dances. Stomped bodies greeted
Phillip Gibbs' red life pouring out while
James Green watched one shot too many.

Factory

It opened out of the ground one day —
subterranean staircase slid you down into the ghost ship
returning, the adult from the cocoon
missing your skeleton, your white larval skins

Some entered it with marks already on the body
but for you, the marks appeared as you worked —
inhaling the chemical glaze brushed on glass
pushing buttons of asbestos down bottled throats

It came home with you, loyal residue collected
on your dark thermos, your steel boots
unlaced in the corner like a punished child

Nighttime your furnace breath puffed like a train
across the river, across other bodies coughing for air
your sulfur lungs burning the bedroom black

Karen Dietrich

Recurring Dream

I can't get the music out of me, the voices singing into my head
          clear bright hands reaching through my body
          me curled inside like a red bean

I feel them hovering the corner of my wet eye, my spirit eye, irisless
          my face in the mirror an upside down outline
          square holes running down me like negative film

I flip a light switch – on, off, on – stare at the clock's hot numbered
   face
          something is chewing the electrical cord, small
          wolf-like, floating up the wall, its mouth sizzling

I'm unable to run, to scream, my legs filled with salt
          there's too much gravity here, it pushes me
          out the open window, down into the street

You leaving again – the backseat always steamed with you
          the car always banking a sharp left into daylight

The Afterward

— following Tranströmer

It is what wraps round us, pale
and inevitable, like an anaconda,
sated   but awaiting   yet another meal.
It is what makes room for us,

takes our names,
gives us well-oiled keys to unfamiliar houses—
       the clapboards we see have new paint.
It beckons us in, gutters the lights.

Then leads us on walks
through gardens filled with long, pointy flowers,
gauzy and iridescent.
Lilies, we think at last,
as their throats close,
petals   dropping   one by one.

It is late afternoon   the hiatal silence
before bats and cicadas begin their whir.
Before shadows
shrink to dark.

Kyle Potvin

Last Bite

Feed me strawberries and cream,
Mostly cream,
And carrots from my garden, the ones
That roast sweet as candy.

Airmail me a French baguette
I can toast for breakfast.
And, please, a gyro and *frites*
From that place in the Latin Quarter.

In fact, bring on the red meat!
What does it matter now?
A rare T-bone — with mushrooms
And spinach on the side —
Like the one we shared at the casino
The night we won
And lost on black.

And yes, I want chocolate:
That dark bar with caramel I craved
But gave away. Such regret.
I am greedy for more
As with good conversation,
The kind that only dies
at dawn.

I can handle the bitter,
The sweet, the salty, the sour.
I'll take what you bring
And devour each bite.

Contributor Biographies

Kazim Ali has worked as a political organizer, lobbyist, and yoga instructor. His books include two volumes of poetry, *The Far Mosque* and *The Fortieth Day,* two novels, *Quinn's Passage* and *The Disappearance of Seth,* and a book of lyric prose, *Bright Felon: Autobiography and Cities. Orange Alert: Essays on Poetry and Art* is forthcoming from the University of Michigan Press in 2010. He is founding editor of the small press Nightboat Books (www.nightboat.org). He teaches at Oberlin College and in the University of Southern Maine's low-residency MFA Program. In 2008 he received a Writers and Friends Award from The Lit, Cleveland's literary association, and in 2009 he received an Individual Excellence Award from the Ohio Arts Council.

Nin Andrews is the author of several books including *The Book of Orgasms, Why They Grow Wings, Any Kind of Excuse, MidlifeCrisis with Dick and Jane, Dear Professor, Do You Live in a Vacuum?* and *Sleeping with Houdini.* Her new book, *Southern Comfort,* is just out from CavanKerry Press.

Lana Hechtman Ayers, originally from New York, makes her home in the Pacific Northwest where she works as a manuscript consultant and writing workshop facilitator. Her latest collections of poetry, *What Big Teeth* (Kissena Park Press, 2010) and *A New Red* (Pecan Grove Press, 2010), focus on a feminist retelling of the Red Riding Hood fairy tale.

Janet Barry is a musician and poet who has lived in New Hampshire for the past 20 years. Her writing has been accepted in a number of publications, including *Aegis, November 3rd Club, Off the Coast, Naugatuck River Review, Compass Rose* and *Canary,* and she has had work included in the anthology *Eating her Wedding Dress: A Collection of Clothing Poems*. Janet received a 2009 Pushcart Nomination for her poem "Winter Barn," and recently had the privilege of being a Poetry-Out-Loud judge.

Tara Betts is the author of *Arc and Hue*. She teaches at Rutgers University and leads community-based workshops. Tara graduated from NEC in 2007. Her work has been published in *Essence, Ninth Letter, Callaloo, Gathering Ground* and many others. Her writing has also been dramatized for the stage in several productions, including Steppenwolf Theater's "Words On Fire" and "Fingernails Across the Chalkboard".

Bhisham Bherwani's poetry volume, *The Second Night of the Spirit*, was published in 2009 by CavanKerry Press. He lives in New York City and is a graduate of the New England College MFA Program in Poetry.

Sylva Boyadjian-Haddad is a poet, writer, and Professor of English and Comparative Literature at New England College in Henniker, New Hampshire. She is the founder and Editor-in-Chief of *Entelechy International/A Journal of Contemporary Ideas*. She was three times nominated for a Pushcart Prize (in 2004, 2007, and 2008). She resides in Concord, New Hampshire.

Martha Carlson-Bradley has published a full-length book, *Season We Can't Resist* (WordTech Editions, 2007), and two chapbooks, *Beast at the Hearth* (Adastra, 2005) and *Nest Full of Cries* (Adastra, 2000). "A" is one of the poems she has written in response to the 1727 edition of the *New England Primer*, which she researched as a creative arts fellow at the American Antiquarian Society.

Lee Ann Brown is the author of *Polyverse* (Sun & Moon Press, winner of New American Poetry Series Award) and *The Sleep That Changed Everything* (Wesleyan University Press), and has been published in many journals and anthologies including, recently, *Ecopoetics, The Asheville Poetry Review*, and *The Best of Fence: The First 9 Years*. She has performed her poetry internationally and is the editor and publisher of Tender Buttons press. Born in 1963 in Saitama-ken, Japan and raised in Charlotte, North Carolina, Lee Ann now lives in both New York City and Marshall, NC, where she and her family are starting a collaborative space for performance and poetry called The French Broad Institute (of Time & the River). She holds an MFA in Creative Writing (Poetry) from Brown University and is currently Associate Professor of English at St. John's University in NYC. She has been visiting faculty at Naropa University, The New School for Social Research, Barnard College, Bard and Miami University in Ohio and is a recipient of grants from the New York Foundation for the Arts, the Center for Arts in Education, The Howard Foundation, and the Fund for Poetry, as well as artist residencies such as Yaddo, The MacDowell Colony, Fondation Royaumont, the Virginia Center for Creative Arts, and Djerassi. Her song cycle The Thirteenth Sunday in Ordinary Time and other readings can be found at the websites PENNSOUND and The Electronic Poetry Center.

Laynie Browne is the author of nine collections of poetry and one novel. Her most recent publications include two forthcoming titles: *The Desires of Letters*, from Counterpath and *Roseate, Points of Gold*, from Dusie Books (both 2010). Other recent titles include: *The Scented Fox*, (Wave Books 2007), *Daily Sonnets* (Counterpath Books, 2007) and *Drawing of a Swan Before Memory* (University of Georgia Press, 2005). Her honors include: winner of the National Poetry Series, of the Contemporary Poetry Series, two Gertrude Stein Awards for Innovative American Poetry, and a recent Pushcart Prize Nomination. Her work has been anthologized recently in *Not For Mothers Only* (Fence Books), *Wreckage of Reason, An anthology of Contemporary Xxperimental Prose by Women Writers*, (Spuytenduyvil), and in *The Reality Street Book of Sonnets* (Reality Street Editions, U.K.). She is one of the directors of the POG reading series Tucson, Arizona. She has taught creative writing at The University of Washington, Bothell, at Mills College in Oakland and at the Poetry Center at the University of Arizona, where she is developing a new a poetry-in-the-schools program for K-5 schools.

Wendy Burk is the author of a poetry chapbook, *The Deer*, and the translator of a book of poems by Tedi López Mills, *While Light Is Built*. Her poems and translations have also appeared in journals including *Tin House, Colorado Review, Terrain.org*, and *EOAGH*. Recent projects include a manuscript of the selected poems of Tedi López Mills and a collaboration with poet Eric Magrane based on National Park Service artist residencies in Michigan, Arkansas, and Florida.

Amanda Cobb's work has appeared (or is forthcoming) in *Arts & Letters, The Georgetown Review, Controlled Burn, Pebble Lake Review* and others. She teaches English at West Virginia University and lives in Morgantown with her family.

Joanna Penn Cooper's poems and short prose pieces have appeared or are forthcoming in the journals *Boog City, Opium, elimae, Ping Pong,* SUPERMACHINE, and *Poetry International*. Her chapbook, *Mesmer*, will be available from Dancing Girl Press in Spring 2010. Joanna earned an MFA from New England College and a Ph.D.

from Temple University, and she lives in New York City, where she is a Postdoctoral Teaching Fellow at Fordham University.

Melinda Harr Curley lives in State College, PA, with her husband, Tim; daughter, Devon; and son, Tanner. She received an undergraduate degree in Liberal Arts from Penn State, as well as an MBA. Later in life, she earned an MFA in poetry from The New England College low-residency program. "Seeds and Sparks" is her first published poem.

Stephan Delbos is a New England-born poet living in Prague, the Czech Republic, where he teaches at Charles University, and the Anglo-American University and edits several literary publications, including *The Prague Revue*. His poetry and essays have appeared most recently or are forthcoming in *Agni*, *Atlanta Review*, *New Letters*, *Poetry International*, *Poetry Salzburg Review*, and *Zoland Poetry*. He received his MFA from the New England College MFA Program in Poetry.

Chard deNiord is the author of three books of poetry, *The Double Truth* (forthcoming from the University of Pittsburgh Press in 2011), *Night Mowing* (The University of Pittsburgh Press, 2005), *Sharp Golden Thorn* (Marsh Hawk Press, 2003), and *Asleep in the Fire* (University of Alabama Press, 1990). His poems and essays have appeared in *The Pushcart Prize*, *New England Review*, *Literary Imagination*, *Harvard Review*, *American Poetry Review*, *Ploughshares*, *The Southern Review* and *Iowa Review*. He is a cofounder of The New England College MFA program in poetry and an associate professor of English at Providence College and lives in Putney, Vermont.

Tenzin Dickyi grew up in the Tibetan refugee community in northern India. She studied at the Tibetan Children's Village school and at Cambridge Rindge and Latin High school in Cambridge where her family moved when she was fourteen. She studied English literature at Harvard University. Currently, she works in the Office of Tibet, New York, as Special Assistant to His Holiness the Dalai Lama's Representative to the Americas.

Karen Dietrich's poems and essays appear in several journals, including *Pank, Monkeybicycle, The Dirty Napkin,* and *Scapegoat Review*. Karen is a graduate of the MFA program at New England College. She currently lives in Pennsylvania.

Jonas Ellerström, born 1958, is a Swedish publisher, writer, translator and art critic. He founded the publishing house ellerströms förlag in 1983. Its list comprises first and foremost poetry and literary essays in translation; ellerströms also publish the poetry magazine *Lyrikvännen*. He has also published two collections of his own poetry, a book of author's portraits and a book on chess. He has edited Swedish volumes of critical essays on James Joyce and Flann O'Brien, and has edited the complete poems of early Swedish modernist poet Vilhelm Ekelund in two volumes for the Swedish Academy's series of contemporary classics. He is currently co-editing with Malena Mörling *Swedish Writers On Writing* to be published by Trinity University Press. In addition, he is working with Malena Mörling on translating a selection of poems by Edith Södergran to be published by Marick Press.

Kathleen Fagley is a 2005 graduate of the New England College MFA program in poetry. She lives in Keene, New Hampshire, with her husband and teaches at Keene State College. Her poetry has appeared in *The Comstock Review, Concrete Wolf, The Poet's Touchstone, Slipstream, Cutthroat, Entelechy International* and most recently in *International Psychoanalysis*. Her poetry can be found online in *The DMQ Review* and *Houston Literary Review* and anthologized in *The 2010 Poets Guide to New Hampshire*. She is a poetry editor for *Amoskeag: The Journal of Southern New Hampshire University*.

Howie Faerstein's poems have appeared in *Great River Review*, *Nimrod*, *The Main Street Rag*, *Cut Throat*, *Mudfish* and on-line in *The Pedestal* and *Dirty Napkin*. He lives in Florence, Massachusetts, and teaches American Literature at Westfield State College. He received an MFA in Creative Writing, Poetry from New England College.

Patricia Fargnoli, the NH Poet Laureate from 2006-2009, is the author of four books and two chapbooks. Her latest book is *Then, Something*, Tupelo Press, 2009. Individual poems have been published recently in such journals as *The Massachusetts Review*, *Ploughshares*, and *Nimrod*.

Roberta Feins was born in New York, and has also lived in North Carolina and (currently) in Seattle. She works as a computer consultant. Roberta received her MFA in poetry from New England College in 2007. She has been published in *Antioch Review, Tea Party, Floating Bridge Review, The Lyric,* and *Five AM*. Roberta is an editor of the e-zine *Switched On Gutenberg* (http://www.switched-ongutenberg.org/)

Adam Fieled is a poet based in Philadelphia. He has released three print books: *Opera Bufa* (Otoliths, 2007), *When You Bit...* (Otoliths, 2008), and *Chimes* (Blazevox, 2009), as well as numerous chaps, e-chaps, and e-books, including *Posit* (Dusie Press, 2007) and *The White Album* (ungovernable press, 2009). He has work in journals like *Tears in the Fence, Great Works, The*

Argotist, Upstairs at Duroc, Jacket, and in the *& Now Anthology* from Lake Forest College Press. A magna cum laude graduate of the University of Pennsylvania, he also holds an MFA from New England College and an MA from Temple University, where he is completing his PhD.

Alice B. Fogel's most recent book of poetry is *Be That Empty*, which was on the national poetry bestseller list for 4 weeks in 2008. A recipient of an Individual Artist Fellowship from the National Endowment for the Arts, her work has appeared in the Best American Poetry series, and many other anthologies and journals. Her 2009 book, *Strange Terrain: A Poetry Handbook for the Reluctant Reader*, is a nonacademic guide for those who don't "get" poetry. Visit her website at www.alicebfogel.com.

Laura Davies Foley is the author of two books of poetry, *Syringa* and *Mapping the Fourth Dimension*. She has won the Atlanta Review Grand Prize and been awarded a Fellowship from Frost Place. Her work has appeared in *Valparaiso Poetry Review, Bloodroot Literary Magazine, California Quarterly, The Georgetown Review, The Distillery* and other print and online journals, and one of her poems has been nominated for a Pushcart Prize. She is currently a chaplain intern with New York Zen Center for Contemplative Care and lives on the wide banks of the Connecticut River in Cornish, NH.

Jacqueline Gens is the co-director and one of the founders of the MFA Program in Poetry at New England College. For many years, she worked at the Naropa Institute (now University) in Boulder, CO, before joining the staff of the late poet, Allen Ginsberg in NYC. She is a regular contributor to a number of Buddhist publications. Her poetry chapbook, *Primo Pensiero*, with a foreword by Anne Waldman, was published by Shivastan Press in the fall of 2008. Poems have been published or are forthcoming in *The Alembic Review*, *Henniker Review*, *Connotations*, *Poetry International*, *Mercy of Tides: Poems for a Beach House* (Salt Marsh Pottery Press), and *The Mirror*.

Mary Gilliland lives in Ithaca, New York, where she serves on the Board of Namgyal Monastery Institute of Buddhist Studies, the Dalai Lama's seat in North America. Her awards include the Stanley Kunitz Fellowship at the Fine Arts Work Center in Provincetown, an Ann Stanford Prize, and a Cornell Council on the Arts Faculty Grant. Recent and forthcoming poetry can be found at http://courses.cit.cornell.edu/mg24/poetry.htm and in *Agni*, *Chautauqua*, *Notre Dame Review*, *Passages North*, *Poetry*, *Seneca Review*, and *Stand*.

Mariela Griffor was born in the city of Concepcion in southern Chile. She attended the University of Santiago and the Catholic University of Rio de Janeiro. She left Chile for an involuntary exile in Sweden in 1985. She and her American husband returned to the United States in 1998 with their two daughters. They live in Grosse Pointe Park, Michigan. She is co-founder of The Institute for Creative Writers at Wayne State University and Publisher of Marick Press. Her work has appeared in periodicals across Latin America and the United States. Mariela Holds a B.A in Journalism and a M.F.A. in Creative Writing from New England College. She is the author of *Exiliana* (Luna Publications) and *House* (Mayapple Press). She is Honorary Consul of Chile in Michigan.

James Harms is the author of seven books of poetry, including the forthcoming *Comet Scar*, to be published by Carnegie Mellon University Press in 2011. He is the recipient of an NEA Fellowship, the PEN/Revson Fellowship and three Pushcart Prizes, among other honors. A Professor of English at West Virginia University, he is also co-director of the MFA Program in Poetry at New England College.

Brian Henry is the author of five books of poetry—*Astronaut* (published in the U.S. and England, where it was short-listed for the Forward Prize, and also published in Slovenia in translation), *American Incident*, *Graft* (published in the U.S. and England), *Quarantine* (winner of the Alice Fay di Castagnola Award from the Poetry Society of America), and *The Stripping Point*—and the chapbooks *In the Unlikely Event of a Water* and *Hit and Run*. His sixth book, *Lessness*, is forthcoming from Ahsahta Press. His poems have appeared in numerous magazines around the world, including *The New Republic, American Poetry Review, The Paris Review, Grand Street, Poetry Review*, and *Jacket*. His poetry has been collected in many anthologies and has been translated into Russian, Slovenian, and Croatian. He has co-edited *Verse* since 1995, and he co-edited *The Verse Book of Interviews*. His poetry criticism has appeared in numerous publications around the world, including *The New York Times Book Review, Times Literary Supplement, Jacket, Boston Review, The Yale Review*, and *Virginia Quarterly Review*. His translation of the Slovenian poet Tomaž Šalamun's *Woods and Chalices* appeared from Harcourt in 2008; he is currently translating Aleš Šteger's *The Book of Things*. He is core faculty in the New England College MFA Program in Poetry.

M.C. Jones
Work has or will appear in *Poetry International, elimae, Naugatuck River Review, Scapegoat Review* and *WebDelSol*. In January, 2010, she was among those selected by New Hampshire Poet Laureate Walter Butts for inclusion in the New Hampshire State Council on the Arts' Poet Showcase. Jones curates the reading series *Datum:*

Earth in Keene, NH. As a creative director and copywriter, her commercial work for clients like Target, Aveda has appeared in design annuals like *Communication Arts, How* and *Print*. Jones received her MFA in July of 2009.

Ilya Kaminsky was born in Odessa, former Soviet Union in 1977, and arrived in the United States in 1993, when his family was granted asylum by the American government. Ilya is the author of *Dancing In Odessa* (Tupelo Press, 2004) which won the Whiting Writer's Award, the American Academy of Arts and Letters' Metcalf Award, the Dorset Prize, the Ruth Lilly Fellowship given annually by *Poetry* magazine. *Dancing In Odessa* was also named Best Poetry Book of the Year 2004 by *ForeWord Magazine*. In 2008, Kaminsky was awarded Lannan Foundation's Literary Fellowship. In 2009, poems from his new manuscript, *Deaf Republic*, were awarded *Poetry* magazine's Levinson Prize. His anthology of 20th century poetry in translation, *Ecco Anthology of International Poetry*, is published by Harper Collins in March, 2010. In addition, Ilya writes poetry in Russian. His work in that language was chosen for "Bunker Poetico" at Venice Bienniale Festival in Italy. In the late 1990s, he co-founded Poets For Peace, an organization which sponsors poetry readings in the United States and abroad with a goal of supporting such relief organizations as Doctors Without Borders and Survivors International. Currently, he teaches Contemporary World Poetry, Creative Writing, and Literary Translation in the Master of Fine Arts Program in Creative Writing at San Diego State University and in the low-residency MFA Program in Poetry at New England College. He lives in San Diego, Califonia with his beautiful wife, Katie Farris.

Talia Katowicz lives in Rhode Island and teaches elementary and middle school art and Spanish.

Anchia Kinard is an MFA student at New England College in Henniker, NH. She specializes in poetry. Prior to grad school, she attended Union College in Schenectady, NY. She graduated with a B.A. in English. Raised in Charlotte, NC, Anchia now lives in Easthampton, MA. Anchia was honored with the 2001 OPUS Literary Award in Charlotte, NC and achieved an Honorable Mention for the 2004 Audre Lorde Poetry Prize in Troy, NY. Her realm of writing has led her to interview such notable figures as Richard Jenkyns, a descendant of Jane Austen and professor at Oxford, Zine Magubane, historian, and the Reverend Jesse Jackson. She is looking forward to developing her writing and distinguishing herself as a poet of substance.

Francesco Levato, poet, translator, and new media artist, is the author of three books of poetry: *Elegy for Dead Languages*; *War Rug*, a book length documentary poem; and *Marginal State*. His translations of the works of Italian poets Tiziano Fratus, *Creaturing*, and Fabiano Alborghetti, *The Opposite Shore*, are forthcoming from Marick Press in the spring and fall of 2010. His work has been published internationally in journals and anthologies, both in print and online, including *Drunken Boat*, *The Progressive*, *Versal*, and many others. His cinépoetry has been exhibited in galleries and featured at film festivals in Berlin, Chicago, New York, and elsewhere.

Sara Lefsyk graduated from the New England College MFA Program in Poetry in 2009. She currently lives and volunteers at The Kripalu Center for Yoga and Health.

Louise Landes Levi Poet, translator, traveler and musician. Studies at UC BERKELEY in the '60s led to a study in depth of Indian music and later to the translation of two major works: *The Love*

Poems of Mira Bai (Cool Grove Press 1997 and 2003) and Rene Daumal's *Rasa* (New Directions 1982 and Shivastan 2003 and 2006) a cult classic on Indian Aesthetics. Following a lineage of beings devoted to the road, to the book and to the equality of beings, her poetry books include: *The Book L* (Cool Grove 2010), *Banana Baby* (Supernova 2006), *Avenue A & 9th Street* (Shivastan 2004), *Chorma* (Porto dei Santi 2000), *Guru Punk*, (Cool Grove Press 1999), *The House Lamps Have Been Lit* (Supernova 1996), *Extinctions*, (Left Hand Books 1993), and *Concerto* (City Lights, Accordian Series, 1988). *Toward Totality* (Vers La Completude) and *Selected Works 1920-1973*, her translations from the French visionary Henri Michaux, was published by Shivastan in 2006. Reviews, essays and poems have been published online at *Arthur, Big Bridge, Jacket, Rain Taxi* and *Unlikely Stories*, among others.

Lesle Lewis' books include *Small Boat* (winner of 2002 Iowa Poetry Prize) and *Landscapes I & II* (Alice James Books 2006). Her new book, *lie down too*, winner of the Beatrice Hawley Award is forthcoming in 2011 (Alice James Books). She lives in New Hampshire and teaches at Landmark College in Vermont.

Barbara P. Lovenheim teaches in the Master of Arts in Liberal Studies Program at Nazareth College, Rochester, NY. She has published poetry in *miller's pond, Hazmat, Scapegoat Review, Free Focus* as well as in the anthologies *Of Risk Courage and Women: Our Different Voices* and *In Other Words: A Poetry Anthology*. Her book review on Nicole Cooley's *The Afflicted Girls* was included on womenwriters.net. She writes a monthly book review of Jewish books called Sfarim.

Terry Lucas has recent or forthcoming work in *Green Mountains Review, OVS,* and *Poets & Artists*. In addition, he has recently launched a new blog (http://www.postpoetrymfa.blogspot.com) and a new community site (http://postpoetrymfa.ning.com) providing resources and support for MFA graduates. Terry is an assistant editor for *Fifth Wednesday Journal* and a guest editor for the spring 2010 issue of *OVS*.

Erika Lutzner hosts a monthly writing salon called Upstairs At Erika's in Brooklyn, NY, as well as runs New Poets For Peace, an organization which holds readings around the nation (more can be found at www.newpoetsforpeace.com). Formerly a professional chef, she edits a quarterly online journal called *Scapegoat Review* and is working on a memoir. Her work can be found in various anthologies such as *Ping Pong* and *Naugatuck River Review* and the online journals *Eclectica, elimae, failbetter, Wicked Alice, Web del Sol,* and *The November 3rd Club*. She also writes for *Poetry International's* weblog.

Maura MacNeil's collection of poems, *A History of Water*, was a top ten finalist in the Finishing Line Press Open Chapbook Competition and published in August 2007. Her poetry has appeared numerous publications and has been anthologized in *The Breath of Parted Lips: Voices from the Frost Place, Volume II* from CavanKerry Press. She is co-founder and editor of *Entelechy International: A Journal of Contemporary Ideas* and a co-founder of the Stone Bridge Poetry Project in Henniker, NH. She teaches at New England College where she is an Associate Professor of Writing.

Tamara J. Madison is a writer, poet, and performer currently living and working in Georgia. Her literary work has been published in various journals and anthologies including: *Temba Tupu!* (2009), an international anthology of poetic portraits of Africana Women published by Red Sea Press, edited by Nagueyalti Warren, PLUCK! A *Journal of Affrilachian Culture,* Tea Party Magazine and *Check The Rhyme, An anthology of female poets and emcees* (nominated for a 2007 NAACP Image Award in Poetry/Literature). Tamara is the author and performer of *Naked Voice,* the 2002 winner of the First Literary Recording Contest sponsored by AUTHENTIC VOICE work Records. She has also written and performed works for stage and television. Tamara has recorded as a bilingual poet and songstress on the self-titled CD, JUBA Collective (Premonition Records), an internationally performing, and multidisciplinary, touring arts ensemble from Chicago. She is currently completing and Master of Fine Arts degree at New England College.

Eric Magrane is the editor of the new experiment *Spiral Orb,* an online journal practicing permaculture poetics [spiralorb.net]. He writes for both the page and for glass and mirror; you can find his permanent mirror-poem installation *only mountains* at Casa Libre en la Solana in Tucson, Arizona. In his day job he is a hiking guide.

Kent Maynard is an anthropologist teaching at Denison University, as well as a student in the low-residency MFA-Poetry Program at New England College. Recent poems appear in *Borderlands, Cold Mountain, The Comstock Review, South Carolina Review, Southern Humanities Review, Sow's Ear Poetry Review,* and *Spoon River.* A chapbook, *Sunk Like God Behind the House,* won the 2000 Open Chapbook Competition for Ohio Poets, and was published by the Wick Program at Kent State University, 2001.

Tim Mayo's poems and reviews have appeared or will appear in *Atlanta Review, Avatar Review, The Brattleboro Reformer, Babel Fruit, 5 AM, Inertia Magazine, Poetry International, Poet Lore, The*

Worcester Review, *Verse Daily*, *Verse Wisconsin* and *The Writer's Almanac*. In 2008 Pudding House Publications published his chapbook *The Loneliness of Dogs*, and his full length collection *The Kingdom of Possibilities* was published in 2009 by Mayapple Press. His poetry has been recognized with two Vermont Studio Center Fellowships and as a finalist for the 2009 Paumanok Award. He is a former member of the Brattleboro Literary Festival and lives in Brattleboro, Vermont, where he substitute teaches in the public schools.

Mary McKeel lives in Charlotte, North Carolina, where she was born and went to school at the University of North Carolina at Chapel Hill and the Paralegal Program at Central Piedmont Community College. Several of her poems have appeared in *Thrift Literary Review*. She won the literary magazine's first prize for poetry at The University of North Carolina at Charlotte.

Stephen Paul Miller is the author of several books including *The Seventies Now: Culture as Surveillance* (Duke University Press), *The Bee Flies in May* (Marsh Hawk Press), *Skinny Eighth Avenue* (Marsh Hawk Press), *Fort Dad* (Marsh Hawk Press), and *Art Is Boring for the Same Reason We Stayed in Vietnam* (Domestic). He co-edited, with Terence Diggory, *The Scene of My Selves: New Work on New York School Poets* (National Poetry Foundation) and, with Daniel Morris, *Radical Poetics and Secular Jewish Culture* (University of Alabama Press). He is a professor of English at St. John's University, and he was a Senior Fulbright Scholar at Jagiellonian University in Krakow, Poland.

Malena Mörling was born in Stockholm and grew up in southern Sweden. She is the author of two books of poetry, *Ocean Avenue*, and *Astoria*. She received a Guggenheim Fellowship in 2008 and is a Research Associate at The School for Advanced Research in Santa Fe, NM. She is currently co-editing the anthology *Swedish Writers On Writing* with Jonas Ellerström, which will be a part of The Writer's World series from Trinity University Press. In addition, she is working with Jonas Ellerström on translating a selection of poems by Edith Södergran to be published by Marick Press. She lives in Santa Fe, NM, and teaches at The University of North Carolina, Wilmington and in the MFA Program at New England College.

Nikoletta Nousiopoulos holds a MFA in Poetry from New England College. Her poems have appeared in *elimae*, *South Jersey Underground*, *2River*, and *Harpur Palate*. She was a 2010 finalist for the Philbrick Poetry Award, and was a winner of the 2009 Dorothy Sargent Rosenberg Poetry Prize. Her first book *all the dead goats* was released in 2010 from Little Red Tree Publishing.

Annmarie O'Connell hails from the south side of Chicago and began writing poetry at an early age. This early interest in poetry eventually led her to attain both a B.A. in poetry from Columbia College Chicago, and an MFA in creative writing at New England College's poetry program. Currently, Annmarie works at a domestic violence shelter counseling women and children.

Ivy Page: After completing an MFA in Creative Writing at New England College, and longing for a creative group of folks to socialize with, Ivy started a literary and art journal (OVS Magazine), and found ways to create a poetry community in the foothills of the White Mountains here in Northern New Hampshire. Her poetry has been published in *Underground Voices*, *The Smoking Poet*, *Boston Literary Magazine*, *The Houston Literary Review*, *New Plains Review*, and *Night Train*, among others. Her book review of Sarah Luczaj's *An Urgent*

Request appears in the current issue of *New Southerner*. Ivy teaches workshops and currently is an adjunct at two colleges.

Barbara Paparazzo lives in Conway, Massachusetts, and has published poetry in the *Atlanta Review, Appalachia Review, Cincinnati Review, Rattle, The Dirty Napkin* and other journals. Her chapbook *The Red Silk Scarf* is forthcoming from Shivastan Publications in spring 2010. She received an MFA in Poetry from New England College in 2005.

Alexandria Peary's first book of poetry, *Fall Foliage Called Bathers & Dancers*, was published in 2008. Poems from her second manuscript are forthcoming in *The Denver Quarterly, New American Writing, Jubilat, Literary Imagination,* and *Verse*. Her poetry has received a Pushcart nomination and has been awarded the Joseph Langland Award from the Academy of American Poets. She has a MFA in Poetry from the University of Iowa ('94) and a second MFA in Poetry from the University of Massachusetts, Amherst ('99). She is finishing her doctorate in Composition at the University of New Hampshire, Durham, and has published articles recently in College Composition and Communication and in the edited collection, Engaging Audience, from NCTE. She is the Writing Program Director and an associate professor at Daniel Webster College in Nashua, NH, where she designs courses on poetry, composition, writing-for-publication, and strategies for overcoming writer's blocks.

Jane Lunin Perel is professor of English and Women's Studies at Providence College. She has published four collections of verse poetry. This poem comes from her most recent work and first manuscript of prose poetry, Red Radio Heart, which is currently seeking a publisher. Her prose poems have appeared in *The Prose*

Poem: An International Journal, *The Best of the Prose Poem: An International Journal*, *Sentence*, *Flights*, and *The Alembic*.

Douglas Piccinnini's writing has recently appeared in *The Cultural Society*, EOAGH, *Lana Turner, mid)rib, So and So, Supermachine* and other journals. He lives in Brooklyn, NY, and curates the CROWD Reading Series.

Verandah Porche works as a poet-in-residence, performer and writing partner around New England. Based in rural Vermont since 1968, she has published *The Body's Symmetry* and *Glancing Off*, and has pursued an alternative literary career, creating collaborative writing projects in nontraditional settings: literacy and crisis centers, hospitals, factories, nursing homes, senior centers, a 200 year-old Vermont tavern and an urban working class neighborhood. Listening Out Loud documents her residency with Real Art Ways in Hartford, CT. She has presented her work on NPR's "Artbeat," NH Public Radio's "Front Porch," in the Vermont State House and at the Guggenheim Museum. The Vermont Arts Council presented her with an Award of Merit, honoring her contribution to the state's cultural life.

Kyle Potvin's poetry has appeared in print and online publications including *The Lyric, Measure, JAMA* (Journal of the American Medical Association), *Literary Mama, The Barefoot Muse, The New York Times'* "Well" blog and The 2008 and 2010 *Poets' Guide to New Hampshire*. She was named a finalist for the 2008 Howard Nemerov Sonnet Award. She is principal of a public relations firm.

George Quasha, artist and poet, explores principles in common within language, sculpture, drawing, video, sound, installation, and performance. His recent *Axial Stones: An Art of Precarious Balance*, foreword by Carter Ratcliff (2006), features work shown at the Baumgartner Gallery (Chelsea), Slought Foundation (Philadelphia), the Samuel Dorsky Museum of Art (SUNY New Paltz), and elsewhere. His video installation work, *art is: Speaking Portraits*, recording over 700 artists, poets, and composers (in 11 countries and 21 languages) saying what art is, has been exhibited internationally at museums, galleries, and universities. Awarded a Guggenheim Fellowship in video art and an NEA Fellowship in poetry, author of 14 books, his *An Art of Limina: Gary Hill's Works and Writings* (with Charles Stein; foreword by Lynne Cooke) has just been published (Poligrafa: Barcelona, 2009). Many of his books (including *Somapoetics, Giving the Lily Back Her Hands*, and *Ainu Dreams*), videos, drawings, sculptures, and critical pieces can be viewed at www.quasha.com. With Susan Quasha, he is founder and publisher of Station Hill Press of Barrytown, New York.

Steven Riel's third chapbook, *Postcard from P-town*, was named runner-up for the 2008 Robin Becker Chapbook Prize and was published by Seven Kitchens Press. Christopher Bursk selected Riel to serve as the 2005 Robert Fraser Distinguished Visiting Poet at Bucks County Community College. He works as a librarian at Harvard University. He is a graduate of the New England College MFA Program in Poetry.

Edith Södergran (1892-1923) was born in St. Petersburg, Russia, and lived in the Swedish-speaking part of southeast Finland. She was a pioneer of free verse and was a distinct and powerful voice in Swedish poetry. Södergran's lyrical poetry was bold and expansive in its vision. A leading European modernist, she was highly regarded by her contemporaries and influenced generations of Swedish poets. Her poetry has shown a remarkable ability to continually speak to new readers and fascinate scholars. She is on par with Else Lasker-Schüler and other early European modernists. Edith Södergran died from tuberculosis at the age of 31.

Leah Souffrant borrows from Samuel Beckett's *Ohio Impromptu* on page130. She lives in Brooklyn, New York. She is a founding co-chair of the Poetics Group at the Graduate Center (CUNY), where she is a Ph.D. candidate. In 2007, she was awarded a New York Foundation for the Arts fellowship in poetry.
Cinnamon Stuckey stems from a mixed cultural bloodline of Chiricahua Apache, Afro-Cuban, Irish and Czechoslovakian. She lives and writes in Sierra Vista, AZ. Currently working on her MBA in Management through Western International University, she is a graduate of New England College with an MFA in Creative Writing (2009).

K. A. Thayer is a PhD Candidate in the Communication and Rhetoric program at Rensselaer Polytechnic Institute. His poetry has been published in *Entelechy International, Caesura, The Alembic, Diner, Paragraph, The Fourth International Anthology on Paradoxism*, and others.

Matthew Ulland is the author of *The Sound in the Corn*, a chapbook from Finishing Line Press. Recent poems and essays appear in *LIT, Hanging Loose, caesura* and other journals. He lives in the woods north of New York City with his partner in a house full of dogs.

Miguel Alejandro Valerio was born in the Dominican Republic in 1985 and moved to the US in 1995. He is currently pursuing an MA in Spanish at St. John's University, New York, where he also did his undergraduate studies, graduating with a BA in Philosophy in the spring of 2008.

Mark Watman is a poet, writer, and Assistant Professor of Writing at New England College in Henniker, New Hampshire. As a poet he has published in both regional and national magazines and journals. He holds a Master of Fine Arts degree in Writing and Literature from the Bennington Writing Seminars at Bennington College.

Dorinda Wegener holds a MFA from New England College where she was a Joel Oppenheimer Award recipient. Her poems have been published or are forthcoming in *The Antioch Review, Indiana Review, Hotel Amerika, Mid-American Review, Sou'wester,* and *The Marlboro Review* Online. She resides in Wilton, NH.

NEW ENGLAND COLLEGE LOW-RESIDENCY MFA PROGRAM IN POETRY

TRADITION & INNOVATION: The first single genre poetry program. A community of writers working together in a collegial program that recognizes the importance of close listening, sharp critical acumen, respectful response, and what Marianne Moore called "**a place for the genuine.**"

Concentrated Studies in:
Performance · New Media
Translation · Prose for Poets
Teaching

Announcing a new MA in Professional Writing – Online:
www.nec.edu/graduate-and-professional-studies/ma-in-professional-writing

Faculty 2009/2010
Carol Frost, James Harms, Brian Henry, Ilya Kaminsky, Paula McLain, Malena Morling, D.A. Powell and Eleni Sikelianos.

New England College

New England College
MFA Program in Poetry
98 Bridge Street
Henniker, NH 03242
603-219-9172

www.nec.edu/graduate-and-professional-studies/mfa-in-poetry

Visit our program blog at
www.tygerburning.blogspot.com

New England College
Post-MFA Poetry Symposium
July 11-15, 2010

Open to poets with an MFA or graduate degree in Creative Writing. Our program includes:

- Small Workshops
- Participant & Faculty Readings
- Manuscript Critiques
- Individual Conferences
- Editorial Advice
- Creative Writing Theory & Pedagogy

Download a pdf brochure and application at:
www.nec.edu/graduate-and-professional-studies/mfa-in-poetry/the-2010-post-mfa-symposium

Our Post-MFA Poetry faculty includes Daisy Fried, Ed Ochester, Neil Shepard, Chard deNiord, Maxine Kumin, Sven Birkerts, Cara Blue Adams, Peter Everwine.

New England College

Post-MFA Program in Poetry
98 Bridge Street • Henniker, NH 03242 • 603-219-1030

Visit the Post-MFA Symposium blog at www.postmfasymposium.blogspot.com

TYGERBURNING LITERARY JOURNAL SUBSCRIPTIONS

One year
Single issue
$15 not including U.S. shipping & handling

Two years
PLUS FREE: Inaugural Issue+1 Marick Press Title
$30 not including U.S. shipping & handling

Three years
PLUS FREE: Inaugural Issue+ 1 Marick Press Title
$45 not including U.S. shipping and handling

Payment can be made by credit card through our online bookstore.

Order via our online bookstore or use the subscription form.

If you prefer to send checks please prints the following form and send it with a check or money order.

Marick Press
Subscription Tygerburning Literary Journal
P.O. Box 36253
Grosse Pointe Farms, MI 48236
(313) 407 9236

TYGERBURNING LITERARY JOURNAL

Stories, poems, essays, and book reviews
Subscription Order Form

I'd like to order one of the following:

3 years (3 issues) of **Tygerburning Literary Journal** for $ 45
2 years (2 issues) of **Tygerburning Literary Journal** for $30
1 year (1 issues) of **Tygerburning Literary Journal** for $ 15

Send subscription to:

Name: _____

Address: _____

_____

Billing address, if different from above:

Name: _____

Address: _____

_____

Is this a gift?
Gift message: _____

_____

Your phone or email address, in case we encounter problems with your order: _____

Please send check or money order payable to *Marick Press* or include your credit card information below. We accept Visa or MasterCard.

Account number: _____

Expiration date: _____

Signature: _____

Mail to:
Marick Press • *Tygerburning Literary Journal* • P.O. Box 36253,
Grosse Pointe Farms, MI 48236 • (313) 407 9236

AN ANNUAL POETRY CONTEST

One first place winner receives $1000 and publication in Tygerburning Literary Journal, Issue #2, Spring 2011! Two honorable mentions receive $100 and publication.

The 2011 judge: Brian Henry

When is the deadline?
The postmark deadline is December 15th, 2010

What are the guidelines?
- $20 entry fee. Make checks payable to "Marick Press"
- Entries must be postmarked by December 15th
- Submit up to three poems, not to exceed six pages.
- Poems must be original, written in English, and previously unpublished
- Your name or address should not appear anywhere on the poems.
- Your name or address should appear only on the cover letter.
- You may submit via electronically or by snail mail.
- If you mail your entry, enclose an index card with poem titles, your name, address, phone number, and email address
- If you mail your entry, enclose an SASE for notification of winners
- You may also enclose a postage-paid postcard for acknowledgement of entry (if you'd like)
- Entries must be typed, and on one side of the paper only
- If using the mail, use a paper clip or send unbound—no staples or binding, please

- Once submitted, entries cannot be altered
- No translations please
- Multiple entries allowed—each entry must include a separate entry fee
- No entries will be returned
- Email jgens@nec.edu for information or questions

To **submit electronically**, please submit only one file as a word attachment, with up to three poems. Email to jgens@nec.edu

To submit via the mail, send to Tygerburning Literary Journal, New England College, MFA Program in Poetry, 98 Bridge Street, Henniker, NH 03242. Include a check for $20.00 payable to "Marick Press" or pay using a credit card on PayPal on Marick Press Website under **Hayden Carruth Poetry Prize**

No former or current students of the judge may enter the contest.

www.ingramcontent.com/pod-product-compliance
Lightning Source LLC
Chambersburg PA
CBHW020854090426
42736CB00008B/367